Endangered Phrases

Endangered Phrases

Intriguing Idioms Dangerously Close to Extinction

Steven D. Price

SKYHORSE PUBLISHING

To the memory of Jess Stein
Lexicographer, phrase-maker, and friend.

Skyhorse Publishing books may be purchased in bulk at special discounts for sales
promotion, corporate gifts, fund-raising, or educational purposes. Special editions can
also be created to specifications. For details, contact the Special Sales Department,
Skyhorse Publishing, 307 West 36th Street, 11th Floor, New York, NY 10018 or
info@skyhorsepublishing.com.

Skyhorse® and Skyhorse Publishing® are registered trademarks of Skyhorse
Publishing, Inc.®, a Delaware corporation.

www.skyhorsepublishing.com

10 9 8 7 6 5 4 3 2 1

Library of Congress Cataloging-in-Publication Data is available on file.
978-1-61608-247-5

Printed in China

Introduction

The success of *Endangered Words*, Simon Hertnon's scholarly but eminently readable collection of rarely heard words, prompted Skyhorse's publisher, Tony Lyons, to invite me to write one for phrases. However, rather than limit its contents to obsolete phrases and expressions that are the linguistic equivalent of embalmed, I was more interested in assembling a less erudite, more nostalgic and sociological book that focused as well on phrases and expressions that were on their way out. Language is organic, and vocabularies change over time. Phrases and expressions are created for a variety of reasons. Many enjoy a certain vogue and then fade into obscurity when circumstances change or another more popular word or phrase comes along. For example, Southern California–born Val-Speak was all the rage forty years ago, but now you'd be hard-pressed to find anyone whose response to an improbable situation is "gag me with a spoon!" (however, like the Dude, "well duh!" abides).

Regionalisms were a large part of our national linguistic panorama. Imaginative as all get-out (New England's "as accommodating as a hog on ice" and the South's "faster than a cat lapping chain lightning"), they started disappearing as migration and mass media caused our speech to become homogenized.

New technologies added to vocabularies. The radio gave us "crystal set" as well as such phrases made popular by radio personalities and shows as "Fibber McGee's closet" and "Quiz Kid." The phonograph produced "broken record" and "flip side." Motion pictures gave us "double feature," "B movie," and phrases from the flicks like "circle the wagons!" From television came "just the facts, Ma'am" and "peanut gallery." (No doubt some of today's computer-generated phrases will stay with us while others will vanish into cyberspace).

Classical education provided many phrases, but as schools stop offering such courses, the phrases are joining Latin as a dead language. A pity, because "between Scylla and Charybdis" and "*O tempora! O mores!*," to cite just two such phrases, enrich anyone's vocabulary.

The advent of political correctness has had an effect on speech. Where once most people didn't think twice about using "Chinaman's chance," "black sheep," and "lawn jockey" or even such a seemingly innocuous phrase as "stew zoo," the overt or implicit racial or gender slurs have just about caused the phrases to disappear, certainly from polite conversations.

One of the pleasures of assembling this book was to test whether a particular phrase was indeed endangered. I did so by bouncing it off younger friends and colleagues, and if the response was a "Huh?" or a blank stare, I knew I was onto something (I quickly stopped following up with "You mean you never heard that one?" which did nothing but confirm my advanced age). Many times came the answer, "Yeah, I've heard it, but I don't know what it means," and that was followed after I explained with "That's cool!"

Speaking of age, as I came across any number of phrases and expressions, I heard in my mind's ear the voices of my parents and grandparents and others of their generation. Other people had the same reaction, and I suspect you will too.

I came across lots of endangered phrases in the course of reading and especially from watching television (thank you, Turner Classic Movies). Many books and cybersources were responsible for leads and contributions. Among the reference works were *Brewer's Dictionary of Fact and Fable*, *A Dictionary of Contemporary American Usage* by Bergen Evans and Cornelia Evans, and *Common Phrases . . . and the Amazing Stories Behind Them* by Max Cryer. Websites included The Phrase Finder (http://www.phrases.org.uk/index.html), Expressions & Sayings (http://users.tinyonline.co.uk/gswithenbank/sayindex.htm), The Dog Hause (for animal phrases) (http://www.doghause.com/idioms.asp), Alpha Dictionary (http://www.alpha dictionary.com/slang/), and two indispensable sites for "wordies": Wordsmith (http://www.wordsmith.org) and The Word Detective (http://www.word-detective.com/).

Then there were the friends and relatives who were kind enough to suggest phrase candidates. Profound appreciation goes to Tony Ard, Mike Cohen, Kathy and Larry Burd, Dr. Jeff Buckner, Linda and Hank Beebe, Mari and Rich Goldman, Mandy Lorraine, Diane Maglaris, Dr. Mitchell Sweet, Melanie Garnett, Judy Goldman, John Sands, Lee Weisel, David Perlmutter, Richard Berleth, Joan and Richard Liebmann-Smith, Margy Danson, Norman Fine, Jim Wofford, Sally Stith Burdette, Pat Daniel, and a particularly deep bow to Betsy Wesman.

Finally, my editor Sara Kitchen's unfailing enthusiasm and keen eye contributed volumes to this volume, for which I am, in a phrase, beyond grateful.

A

above the salt (see below the salt)

❧

as accommodating as a hog on ice: very disagreeable.

An old New England expression that imparts a very clear message: swine don't like being very cold any more than people do.

❧

"As the actress said to the bishop . . .": a phrase used to point out or emphasize that a remark had a risqué double meaning, whether or not it was intended.

The phrase, first heard in Britain in the mid-20th century, contrasts a worldly actress and a very proper clergyman to whom such double meanings had to be pointed out. It also took the form of "as the bishop said to the actress," "as the schoolmaster said to the schoolgirl," and any number of other combinations.

Mae West's repartees, such as replying to a man's saying, "I've heard so much about you" with "Yeah, but you can't prove it," coming from almost anyone else would qualify for an "As the actress said to the bishop . . ."

Achilles' heel: a vulnerable spot that leads to a downfall.

According to Greek mythology, anyone who was immersed in the River Styx, which marked the boundary of the underworld, became invulnerable. Thetis dipped her young son Achilles in the river, but she held him by his heel. Because her hand covered that part of his body, the water did not touch it and it became his one vulnerable spot. Achilles, who grew to become a great warrior, died during the Trojan War when an arrow struck his heel.

Even though it's located in the same part of the body, don't confuse "Achilles' heel" with "Achilles tendon," which connects muscles in your lower leg to your heel bone.

Adam's ale: a jocular term for water, based on the strong likelihood that Adam hadn't discovered anything stronger (and they call the Garden of Eden a paradise?). Apparently no fans of alliterations, Scots used to refer to water as "Adam's beer."

⁂

Adam's off ox: an unrecognizable person or thing.

"I wouldn't know him from Adam's off ox" was the equivalent of the contemporary "I wouldn't know him from a hole in the ground."

Since horses and other beasts of transportation and burden are handled from the left side, the left side is referred to as their "near side" and the right side their "off" side. Not to be able to distinguish between someone and the farther-away animal of the first man on Earth is indeed not too know very much at all about a person.

⁂

albatross around one's neck: a burden or stigma brought on by one's actions.

Sailors considered the albatross bird to be an omen or manifestation of good luck, and to harm one was to invite disaster not only to the shooter or trapper but the entire ship's company.

In Samuel Taylor Coleridge's poem "The Rhyme of the Ancient Mariner," the ship's captain killed one such bird that had landed on the deck while the ship was becalmed. When the wind continued to stay away, the crew blamed the captain's action for the bad luck, and he was forced to wear the albatross's carcass around his neck as a reminder of his misdeed.

all hands to the pumps: help!

The phrase comes from sailing days when a leak in the hull required immediate help in bailing out the incoming seawater. A variant is "all hands and the cook on deck," meaning the entire ship's roster was needed in an emergency, even the cook, who was never expected to participate in mariner activities.

all tuckered out: exhausted.

"Tucker" was a 19th-century New England word for "tire" or "used up."

"All-y all-y oxen free!" (also said as "olly olly in-come-free"): it's safe to return home.

This hide-and-seek and kick-the-can game catchphrase assures players that they can return to the starting point without penalty.

Generations of mothers summoned children home to supper by standing on the porch and yelling the phrase.

❧

animal, vegetable, or mineral?
"20 Questions" was a popular parlor game in which players tried to guess the answer by asking no more than twenty questions. The person who answered the questions gave the players the initial hint of whether the subject was animal, vegetable, or mineral.

The game's becoming the format of a very successful radio and then television quiz show beginning in the early 1940s spread the opening hint into general use. Anyone who innocently began a query with "I have a question" was liable to be met with "Is the answer animal, vegetable, or mineral?"

❧

another coat of paint: the narrowest of margins.
The phrase was used in such instances as a ballplayer's commenting that "that pitch came awfully close," to which the batter replied, "Yeah, another coat of paint, and I'd have been a goner."

❧

any port in a storm: assistance or refuge in a predicament especially an unpalatable one.
The metaphor is of sailors happy for any place of safety whatsoever when dangerous weather comes up.

apple-knocker: a country bumpkin.

One of the many terms that city slickers applied to less sophisticated rural dwellers ("rube," "hayseed," and "Gomer" are others). The phrase came from fruit harvesters using long sticks to dislodge the hanging crop.

apple of my eye: a most favorite or cherished person.

In Psalm 17:8, the Psalmist asks God to "keep me as the apple of your eye."

apple pie order: neat, orderly, well organized.

Although the exact derivation is unknown, folk etymology (which word detectives fall back on when there's nothing more authoritative) suggests the following:

New England housewives were so organized at slicing apples for their pies, laying out the slices inside the crust, and then making sure that the top and bottom crusts were evenly pinched together that their meticulousness gave rise to the phrase.

après moi le deluge: a disaster will follow.

The French phrase, translated as "After me the deluge," has been attributed to King Louis XVI or to his mistress, Madame de Pompadour. He or she was referring to the centuries of excessive living enjoyed by the aristocracy and paid for by the rest of France and what would happen as a result when His Majesty (or Madame) went to their heavenly rest. Whether the king or his main squeeze was predicting a cataclysm or simply indicating that he or she didn't care what came after them isn't clear.

Nevertheless, whoever spoke the words was a prophet in his or her time: fourteen years after Louis's death came the revolution that swept away the old order, including Louis's son.

No one could have been ideologically further from the Bourbon monarchy than Karl Marx, who repeated the phrase in his *Das Kapital*: "*Après moi le déluge!* is the watchword of every capitalist and of every capitalist nation. Hence capital is reckless of the health or length of life of the labourer, unless under compulsion from society."

The phrase is the very appropriate motto of Britain's Royal Air Force 617 Squadron, nicknamed "the Dam Busters" for its sorties against German dams during World War II.

~✦~

around the block [also, around the track]: very experienced.

The phrase can be used in two ways. In its nonpejorative sense, you might say, "After all her residencies and years at the hospital, she's been around the block in emergency medicine." On the other hand, to say of a woman that she's been around the block more than a few times suggests that she's of what used to be called "easy virtue."

~✦~

Artful Dodger: a sly person, especially one involved in dubious or criminal activities.

It was the nickname of Jack Dawkins, a young pickpocket in Charles Dickens's *Oliver Twist*. The character survives in the stage and movie musical *Oliver!*, which was based on the Dickens novel, but the phrase as applied to a "sneaky Pete" is now rarely if ever heard.

"Dodger" in the sense of evading danger inspired the name of the Brooklyn (now Los Angeles) baseball team; in its early years in Brooklyn, the team was the "Trolley Dodgers." Brooklyn had many streetcar lines, and to play in the streets required youngsters to dodge streetcars, and "trolley dodger" became the slang term for anyone from that borough.

at bay: to keep someone or something at a safe distance.

The phrase derives from stag hunting, from a French word that also is the source of the English word for the baying howl that hounds make during a chance. A tired and cornered stag that turns to face the pursuing hounds is, for the moment, at a safe distance from its attackers.

❧

at sixes and sevens: in complete disorder.

The most likely source of the phrase is an old dice game called hazard, in which to bet on *cinque* and *sice* (from the French words for "five" and "six") was particularly risky business. Anyone who did so was considered careless or confused. English-speaking players misheard or chose to pronounce *cinque* and *sice* as "sixes and sevens."

❧

B

B movie: the low-budget second part of a movie theater's double feature.

Back in the days of double features, movie houses showed two very distinct types of films. A movies were the hits—"Gone With the Wind," "Casablanca," "Citizen Kane," "The Wizard of Oz"—the ones that drew patrons to the movie houses. Then there were Westerns, horror flicks, and science fiction movies that didn't cost very much to make (they were often in black-and-white). These B movies tended to be shown before the main feature; otherwise, people would leave after the A picture and then feel they hadn't gotten their admission money's worth.

As double features disappeared and the cost of filmmaking grew, the curtain went down on the B movie genre.

✧

get your bait back: just about recoup your expenditure.

An old New England fisherman's expression for barely making expenses. Some who caught just enough fish to sell to compensate for the day's expenses was said to have gotten his bait back.

✧

ball and chain: marriage. A jocularly rueful term for marriage or one's wife.

There was a time when men were supposed to regard marriage in general and their own married state in particular with a certain amount of resignation. The nights of going out drinking with the guys were over, to be replaced by the days of cleaning the attic, painting the garage, and fixing the toilet drip. Marriage was prison (albeit with privileges), wives were wardens, and husbands wore a metaphorical ball and chain, the sort that prisoners wore to prevent escaping.

A young man asked whether he and his girlfriend had wedding plans might reply, "Naw, I'm too young to wear a ball and chain." That reply would rarely be uttered with impunity in the presence of women.

❧

balling the jack: to move rapidly.

A "jack" was a railroad term for locomotive. "Ball" referred to the round electric signal that indicated the speed at which a train should travel. The fastest speed indicated by the signal was at its highest point, which indicated to an engineer that his locomotive could "highball it down the line." Other trainmen would say the engineer was "balling the jack."

The phrase came into general usage from a 1913 ragtime song of the same name. The lyrics gave instructions to do a similarly named dance ("First you put your two knees close up tight, you swing 'em to the left and then you swing 'em to the right . . .").

banana oil: insincere or ridiculous talk.

Like "horse feathers," there's no such substance as banana oil. Also like "horse feathers," the phrase described something utterly preposterous. It has been attributed to Milt Gross, a cartoonist who first used the expression in his comic strips during the 1920s.

bar sinister: a coat of arms ornamentation that is supposedly a sign of illegitimacy. The phrase, which has appeared in the works of novelists Laurence Sterne and Sir Walter Scott, implies a "bar" that prevents the person from a legitimate claim or inheritance, while "sinister" (the heraldic term for a coat of arms' left side) sounds menacing.

Although the idea of a bar sinister on an illegitimate person's shield entered popular speech more than two centuries ago, that's not heraldically correct. A patterned border around a shield was the British heraldry way of indicating bastardy, and if you want to be even more technical, a thin diagonal line that does not touch the edges of the shield is a "baton," not a "bar." However, people rarely check with the College of Arms before using words and phrases.

doesn't know beans: ignorance.

The New England uncomplimentary description of a Bostonian who's so ignorant that he or she can't even cook the city's most famous dish of baked beans spread to the rest of the country.

ॐ

beat around the bush: to speak evasively or misleadingly, or to stall or waste time.

To flush pheasants and other birds so they could be shot, British gamekeepers hired beaters who would swing sticks at likely places where the birds might be lurking. Not to go directly to such foliage but to work around it instead gave the impression of wasting time or not trying very hard to raise the birds; hence, beating around the bush.

ॐ

Beau Brummel: a male fashion plate.

George Bryan Brummel, nicknamed "Beau" was one of the best-known figures of Regency England of the late 18th to early 19th century. As unofficial fashion advisor to the Prince Regent, later King George IV, Brummel was the arbiter of taste, style, and etiquette; he popularized trousers (instead of knee breeches) with matching coats, as well as cravats that were the forerunners of neckties.

The epithet Beau Brummel was applied to any man who was fastidious about his clothing, even if he wasn't a trendsetter.

❧

bee's knees: something that's excellent.

This nonsensical phrase that was popular in the 1920s was, like "the cat's whiskers," the equivalent of today's "really cool" or "it's amazing!" It went the way of such faddish expressions, which is to say, out.

❧

beg the question: to assume the question in your answer.

For example, if the question is "Should marijuana use be criminalized?" to reply "Yes, because if it isn't, then lots of criminals will be roaming the streets" is to beg the question. That is, the answer assumes that pot users are criminals when that's the precise question under debate.

Although the phrase is now widely heard as a synonym for raising or asking a question, its original meaning is still used by the dwindling band of educated speakers.

❦

behind the eight ball: in a precarious situation.

In certain games of pool or billiards, a player whose cue ball (the ball that strikes the other balls) is behind the 8 ball is unlikely to make any shot. Therefore, to be behind the eight ball is to be in a losing situation.

❦

bell the cat: to put yourself in a dangerous position.

The phrase comes from one of Aesop's fables: The Mice held a general council to consider what measures they could take to outwit their common enemy, the Cat. After a general discussion, a young Mouse rose to present a proposal. "You will all agree," he said, "that our chief danger consists in the sly and treacherous manner in which the enemy approaches us. Now, if we could receive some signal of her approach, we could easily escape. I venture, therefore, to propose that a small bell be procured, and attached by a ribbon round the Cat's neck. By this means we should always know when she was about, and could easily retire while she was in the neighborhood."

This proposal met with general applause, until an old Mouse rose to ask, "That is all very well, but who is to bell the Cat?" The Mice looked at one another, but none spoke, whereupon the old Mouse smiled and commented, "It is easy to propose impossible remedies."

belle of the ball: the most appealing woman at a dance or another social occasion.

"Ball" refers to a formal dance, at which there was usually one female who was the cynosure of all male eyes. At other occasions too—case in point: Scarlett O'Hara at the barbecue at Tara where men fell all over themselves to fetch her a plate of food. Fiddle-dee-dee indeed.

below the salt: less socially acceptable, socially inferior.

Due to the difficulty of production in cold climates, salt was an expensive and exclusive commodity in medieval England. At that time, the nobility sat at the dining hall's "high table" whereas their servants and other commoners ate at lower trestle tables. Dishes or containers of salt were placed on the high table where only people of sufficient social rank had access to them.

To be "below [or beneath] the salt" came to mean being less well regarded than other people.

between Scylla and Charybdis: facing the dilemma of two dangerous positions.

Homer's *Odyssey* tells us about two sea monsters that occupied opposite banks of the Strait of Messina between the island of Sicily and mainland Italy. Scylla had six heads that ate sailors who passed too close. Charybdis expelled sea water to create whirlpools that capsized ships that sailed too close. Faced with that option, Odysseus chose to sail toward Scylla and lose only a few crew members rather than risk Charybdis's whirlpool capsizing the ship and drowning everyone (including himself).

As classical education waned and fewer and fewer people understood who Scylla and Charybdis were (hot-house plants? sexually transmitted diseases?), the phrase was replaced by the similar but far less esoteric "between the devil and the deep blue sea."

※

beyond the pale: A pale, originally a stockade made of pales of wood, was an area under the authority of a certain official. In the 14th and 15th centuries the British ruled Dublin, the surrounding area was outside the law. Anyone or anything beyond the pale was considered savage and dangerous, and the express came to mean anything unacceptable or beyond the limits of accepted morality or conduct.

big cheese: a very important person.

The phrase seems to have come from, literally, a very large wheel of cheese. After President Jefferson was given one of Cheshire in 1802, other dairies made and displayed huge wheels for publicity purposes. The cheeses attracted lots of attention, and so it wasn't much of a jump to referring to someone who attracted attention as a "big cheese."

Although some have suggested that "cheese" came from the Hindu word "chiz," for "thing" that the British heard as "cheese," no paper trail exists to show that Americans started using the phrase though any transatlantic connection.

Similar "big" phrases are more common, such as big deal and big wheel.

big hat, no cattle: all talk and nothing to back it up.

"Big hat" is the Western ten-gallon variety; the term is often applied to ranchers. On the theory that if you're going to wear one, you'd better be a cowboy and not just dress like one, you should be able to produce a head or more of livestock. If you couldn't, you were just full of hot air.

bill and coo: to hug and kiss.

A sweet old-fashioned phrase for necking, making out, smooching, or playing kissy-face—the way that courting birds touch bills and emit soft cooing noises before they get down to the real mating game.

bite the bullet: to bear up in an unpleasant or a difficult situation.

In the days before anesthesia, a wounded soldier about to undergo surgery was given a bullet to clamp in his teeth and bear down on so he wouldn't bite off his tongue from the pain.

birthday suit: wearing no clothes.

People said to be in their birthday suit are as naked as the day they were born.

black as pitch: totally dark, without any illumination.

Distilling coal, peat, and other organic substances yield a very dark resinous residue called pitch ("pitch" and "tar" have became virtually synonymous). Anything that dark made a very good simile for "black." The contemporary expression is "pitch black." Those who chose to give the absence of light a theological cast would have said "black as sin," while an imaginative Irish simile was "as black as the Earl of Hell's waistcoat."

∽

black sheep: a disreputable or unloved family member.

Since the majority of domestic sheep have white fleece, a black one would be different from the rest of the flock. And because the word "black" has a historically strong negative connotation, one of that color would be unwanted (in real life, sheep farmers don't like them because black fleece, which can't be dyed, is less commercially valuable).

In the age of politically correct speech, the phrase is now infrequently used, and that's not because family members now get along in greater harmony than they once did.

∽

blanket fever: a lumberjack expression for laziness, as if the woodsman had a medical reason for staying in bed instead of working.

❦

a blot on the escutcheon: bringing dishonor or shame to oneself and one's family.

"Escutcheon" is the heraldic term for the shield on which a family's coat of arms is painted. One with a blot, in the sense of blemish, would look as though there were something wrong, which is what the phrase is meant to convey. When Uncle Fred was hauled off to jail for embezzlement, he not only disgraced himself, he brought shame to his wife, his children, and any living parents. His crime was thus a metaphorical blot on the family escutcheon.

❦

blue movie: a pornographic film.

Why off-color movies were called "blue" remains a matter of conjecture. Although one definition of "blue" has been "lewd" since the 19th century, its application to movies might have referred to the 19th-century Blue Laws morality codes and state and local laws based on them, of which dirty movies would certain run afoul. Other explanations include the bluish tint of the early cheaply made black-and-white movies, and the bluish cigarette and cigar smoke haze in rooms where men gathered to watch such films (the get-togethers were in fact known as "smokers").

"Blue" faded over the years and was replaced by "dirty movie, "adult film," "skin flick" and "hard- or soft-core porn."

∽

blow a fuse: lose your temper.

Back in the days before circuit breakers, a house's electrical system was regulated by a fuse box. Individual fuses connected to separate lines throughout the house were inserted into the box. When a circuit became overloaded, a thin metal strip in the fuse melted, breaking the circuit to prevent an overload and a possible fire. You'd then replace the fuse after disconnecting whatever appliance might have caused the overload.

Someone who because very angry was said to blow a fuse, which doesn't make sense because a fuse was meant to defuse, so to speak, the situation. But no one ever said that idioms must be rational.

Similar expressions that make more sense are "blow your stack," which came from the era of steam engines that would explode if the steam wasn't allowed to explode, and "have a meltdown," as in a nuclear reactor gone wild.

∽

boarding house reach: table manners in which manners were sacrificed for survival.

Most cities and towns have boarding or rooming houses, large private dwellings whose owners took in paying guests who usually stayed for relatively long periods of time.

Dinners were served family style, with boarders joining the owners. If you were one of a large number of people, the choicest or largest amounts of food might be gone by the time the platters reached where you were sitting. And so, disregarding the good manners that you learned at home, rather than wait your turn or asking politely, you reached across the table—and often across your neighbors—to grab serving platters. That arm extension was known as a "boarding house reach."

⌥

bobby soxer: a typical teenage girl of the 1940s and '50s.

Fashion for teenage girls of those decades dictated short white anklets with turned-down tops. Absent any record of an eponymous Bobbi (short for Barbara or Roberta), the best guess about the name is "bob" in the sense of "cut short."

Girls who wore them were known as bobby soxers. When they weren't swooning over Frank Sinatra, they congregated at malt shops or rode in their boyfriends' hot rods. Watching a rerun of the TV show *Happy Days* will put that era in focus.

make no bones about: to speak frankly and directly.

A form of this expression was used as early as the 15th century and meant "without difficulty." The reference is to the bones in stews or soup. Soup without bones would offer no difficulty, and accordingly, one would have no hesitation in swallowing soup with no bones.

pull yourself up by your bootstraps: to succeed through hard work.

Before zippers made getting into tall boots less of a chore, such footwear had leather attachments by which the wearer would pull them on (Western boots and some English riding dress boots still have them).

Trying to raise yourself off the ground by pulling on your bootstraps sounds impossible . . . and it is (don't try it—you'll throw out your back). Therefore to pull yourself up by your bootstraps is to achieve your goals through as much hard work as levitating yourself would take.

born with a silver spoon in his or her mouth: financial and social advantages from family connections.

It was traditional when a child was christened for the godparents to give a silver spoon as a gift or as soon afterwards as they could afford one (if they ever could). However, a child born into a wealthy family always received one at the ceremony. Such infants so privileged were said, often enviously, to have been "born with a silver spoon in their mouth," and the image followed them throughout their lives.

❧

bet your bottom dollar: risk your all your assets.

"Bottom dollar" was the last amount of money in a gambling game stake. If you lost it, you were flat-out broke. Therefore, someone who said that you could bet your bottom dollar on something was telling you that it was a certainty.

And sometimes it was.

❧

like a broken record: to repeat and repeat ad nauseam.

Vinyl records, as those readers who remember them will recall, have spiraling grooves in which the phonograph needle picked up the sound. When a groove developed a crack or other imperfection, the needle became stuck and the sound kept repeating until someone moved the phonograph arm to the next groove.

The expression was applied to anyone who repeated a remark or request over and over until it sounded like a broken record . . . a broken record . . . a broken record.

⌘

Bronx cheer: a raucous expression of displeasure.

The sarcastic reference is to how spectators at sporting events in New York City's borough of the Bronx—at Yankee Stadium, for a notable example—let players on visiting teams, and umpires too, know what was on their mind. The classic "Bronx cheer" sound was produced by compressing the lips and blowing, which replicated the sound of passing wind. That noise was earlier called a raspberry (or raspberry tart, the British rhyming slang for "fart"), from which the word "razz" came.

⌘

bull in a china shop: clumsily destructive.

An early written example of the expression appeared in Frederick Marryat's 1834 novel, *Jacob Faithful*, although the image of a bull wrecking havoc as he wandered among tables and shelves of fine porcelain can be traced a century earlier. The expression can also be found in several European languages, although the animal in question is an elephant.

In 1940, an American press agent led a bull through a New York City china shop as a publicity stunt. The bull didn't break anything, but a bystander trying to avoid the bull backed into a table and caused the damage.

ॐ

bull session: an informal discussion.

A bull session was originally a late-night college men's dormitory conversation with a wide range of topics—politics, sex, sports, sex, religion, sex . . . The word "bull," which meant something boastful or outlandish, came from—no surprise here, "bullshit."

ॐ

bum's rush: a forcible ejection.

The "classical" bum's rush was a bartender or bouncer lifting the deadbeat or intruder by the back of his shirt or jacket collar and the seat of his pants and then throwing him through the tavern door. The phrase, which came into vogue around the turn of the 20th century, survives in its "throw the bum out!" incarnation.

ॐ

bum steer: misleading advice.

This phrase has nothing to do with a tough piece of steak. "Bum" signifies "wrong" and "steer" means "direction" in the sense of steering a vehicle. So if someone has given you a bum steer, you have in a sense grounds for a beef.

⟨❧⟩

burn the candle at both ends: extreme effort without time to rest.

The phrase, which came originally from a French expression, came to mean working so hard that you burn yourself out. In addition, because candles were once an expensive item, to burn one at both ends implied wasting valuable resources to achieve an obsession.

The poet Edna St. Vincent Millay used the image in her verse:

My candle burns at both ends;
It will not last the night;
But ah, my foes, and oh, my friends—
It gives a lovely light.

⟨❧⟩

bury the hatchet: to make peace, to settle differences.

The phrase comes from the practice among native American and Canadian tribes literally to bury a war axe at the end of hostilities.

An 1680 report describes European colonists in what became New England: "Meeting wth ye Sachem [the tribal leaders] the[y] came to an agreemt and buried two Axes in ye Ground; which ceremony to them is more significant & binding than all Articles of Peace . . ."

෧

bush league: anything amateurish or otherwise below professional caliber.

Baseball teams have been divided into two broad categories. Major league teams, also known as the big leagues, have the most professional players who play in state-of-the-art stadiums. Then there are minor league teams, composed of players on their way up or down the baseball ladder and ballparks that range in quality from almost-major league to close-to-sandlot. The latter fields, especially those in rural areas, weren't always enclosed by fences; instead they had shrubbery around their perimeters. Hence the phrase "bush league," where the level of play was far from major league ability.

The expression quickly spread to any endeavor that was less than expertly done.

෧

buy the farm: die

This phrase comes from the military: members of the armed forces were issued insurance policies. Many servicemen speculated that when they returned to civilian life, they would buy a farm back home or pay off the mortgage on one that they or their parents owned. To die was literally to retire, and so combat victims were said to have "bought the farm."

Other phrases that mean "to die" are "cash in your chips" (as if checking out of a poker game), "fall off the perch" (an expiring caged bird), and "go South" (someone now living up North returning to his or her native soil).

‹❧›

by hook or by crook: by any means necessary to accomplish the purpose; one way or another.

Several explanations for this phrase have come down over the years. One is that it refers to two Irish towns, Hook Head and Crook, through which Oliver Cromwell tried to capture the nearby city of Waterford. Another is a medieval custom of allowing villagers to collect for firewood any loose branches that they could pull down with a long-handled curved implement.

A third explanation is the most plausible: shepherds rounded up their flocks by means of a crook, a long staff with a curved end. A shepherd would chase after a reluctant ram, ewe, or lamb and hook it with his staff by any means . . . by hook or by crook.

C

Caesar's wife: a woman whose ethics should not be questioned.

A Roman emperor's wife was deemed to be above reproach; if her morals were called in question, it was a serious problem to her husband's image and political and social power. The phrase came down over the centuries to be applied to any woman, married to a leader or not, whose behavior was—or should be—beyond criticism. (According to the historian Suetonius, what Julius Caesar actually said translates as "My wife should be as much free from suspicion of a crime as she is from a crime itself.")

❧

café society: the collective term for socialites and movie celebrities who frequented fashionable restaurants and nightclubs.

From the end of World War I through the 1960s, the media covered the comings and goings of members of Society (with a capital *S*, the word referred to people of "good family," which in turn meant old money), and glamorous movie stars much as celebrity-chroniclers now report on Paris Hilton, Brad/Angelina, TV reality show personalities, and other boldface celebrities. Among the more popular haunts were Manhattan's Stork Club and El Morocco nightclubs.

Then as now, a substantial portion of the population was interested in the lives of their social betters, and newspaper gossip columnists reported on party- and club-goers in the next day's editions. It was one such scribe, Maury Paul (pen-name: Cholly Knickerbocker) who coined the phrase "café society."

❧

the cards beat all the players: you can't win 'em all.

A fatalistic phrase which tells us that destiny—in the form of a randomly shuffled deck of playing cards—has ultimately the upper hand, no matter how skillful a player might be.

❧

CARE package: a gift parcel.

CARE, the Cooperative for Assistance and Relief Everywhere, was an organization that sent more than 100-million cartons of foodstuffs to war-torn Europe from the end of World War II through 1962.

The phrase was picked up by soldiers, college students, and sleepaway-camp campers for any gift of goodies they received by mail from home.

❧

carriage trade: the best customers.

Restaurants, stores, and other establishments were especially pleased to serve wealthy customers who arrived and departed in their own private horse and carriage, as distinguished from people who came and went by foot or public transportation. It was the purchasing power of the carriage trade that produced a reaction from the establishment's personnel that was solicitous to the point of obsequiousness.

⁓

carry a torch: to love someone, often secretly, who doesn't reciprocate the feeling.

The torch of the phrase could mean the flame of love or a handheld flame that lights the way to spy on the object of your affection, who is probably with his or her current flame.

⁓

the cat that ate the canary: happy, often in a self-satisfied way.

Someone who was very pleased—and often smug—was compared to a house cat that figured out a way to liberate a pet bird from its cage and enjoy the aftermath.

the cat's pajamas: a terrific thing.

This was a nonsensical phrase of the 1920s that meant something worth seeing or having. A similar phrase was the "cat's meow."

Some Other "Cat" Phrases

keep no more cats than can catch mice: use the bare minimum.

A old expression that cautioned against maintaining any more people or things than can accomplish a purpose.

as much chance as a wax cat in hell: a New England expression meaning no chance at all.

cat on a hot tin roof: a Southernism that meant someone who was on edge or nervous. The phrase survives as the title of Tennessee Williams's 1955 Pulitzer Prize–winning drama.

faster than a cat lapping chain lightning: another old Southern expression, this one meaning very fast indeed.

catbird seat: an enviable position, "sitting pretty."

Catbirds seek the highest limbs of trees on which to perch. The view from on high and the relative safety from predators puts them in an advantageous spot. The term is best known as the title of a James Thurber short story and from radio sportscaster Walter Lanier "Red" Barber's using it while broadcasting baseball games.

❧

catch lightning in a bottle: try to do something that's impossible.

The phrase has been attributed to the baseball manager Leo Durocher, who may have originated or simply liked to use it. In any event, it's an apt metaphor for something that no one can do (unless "lightning" refers to lightning bugs, another name for fireflies).

❧

chalk and cheese: two objects that although appearing to be similar are in fact different.

Just as certain varieties of crumbly white cheese might at first glance resemble chalk, so for example, siblings who resemble each other might have completely different personalities. They would be said to be as different as chalk and cheese.

cherchez la femme: This French phrase that translates as "look for a woman," originated with the elder Alexandre Dumas in his novel *The Mohicans of Paris*. Its meaning is that unusual male behavior can often be traced to involvement with a female.

For example, countless generations of adolescent boys who never paid attention to their wardrobe or personal grooming suddenly became interested in clothing fashions. They washed their face and combed their hair without being told to, and spent hours chatting on the telephone (now a computer or handheld device) with the classic teenage boy's dreamy/dopey look on their face. Their parents would regard the phenomenon with a knowing and bemused expression as they told each other, "*cherchez la femme.*"

cheese it—the cops!: a warning that the police were coming.

"Cheese" might be a variant of "cease." It might also come from the cheese course coming at the end of dinner; in the sense that with nothing else ahead, it's time to leave.

In either event, "cheese it—the cops!" was a staple of mid-20th-century crime novels and films, as well as such movies as *The Dead End Kids* and *The Bowery Boys*.

Cheshire cat: having a perpetual, mischievous grin, one that is often indistinguishable from smugness.

Although the Cheshire cat is best known as a character in Lewis Carroll's *Alice's Adventures in Wonderland*, it appeared much earlier in popular English culture, so the phrase may have originally referred to cheese made in the country of Cheshire and molded roughly to resemble a grinning cat.

Lewis Carroll's feline had the ability to disappear until only its smile remained. The cheese variety would be sliced from hind end to front, which similarly gave the impression that its smile—if cheese showed emotion—would be the last to go.

like a chicken with its head cut off: in a frenzy.

Chickens have been known to twitch and even stagger around for several minutes after being decapitated, the result of a reflexive response. A person in the throes of extreme emotional agitation exhibits the same sort of fowl play.

one day chicken and the next day feathers: a Southern expression reflecting that sometimes you have something valuable or what you wished for, but other times you don't.

⁂

a chicken in every pot: prosperity.

The phrase came from a newspaper advertisement by the Republican National Committee during Herbert Hoover's 1928 presidential campaign. The ad pointed out that the preceding administrations of presidents Warren Harding and Calvin Coolidge had "put the proverbial 'chicken in every pot.' And a car in every backyard, to boot." Although credited with the statement, Hoover never promised "a chicken in every pot."

In a similar vein, King Henry IV of France vowed on his coronation in 1589 that "if God grants me the usual length of life, I hope to make France so prosperous that every peasant will have a chicken in his pot on Sunday." His assassination in 1610 at age fifty-seven stymied such a plan.

⁂

Chinaman's chance: slim to no possibility.

There have been several explanations about the origin of this odious phrase, all arising from Chinese immigrants working in the American West. One is that they were given the most dangerous jobs, such as setting and igniting explosives. Another is that judges and juries routinely convicted Chinese defendants on the flimsiest of evidence. A third is that Chinese miners were allowed to work gold claims only after others had taken the best ore.

In any event, "Chinaman's chance" should be relegated to the slag heap.

cଥୁ

Chinese fire drill: a politically incorrect term for chaos.

The phrase supposedly originated in the early 1900s. A ship with British officers and a Chinese crew practiced an engine room fire drill. The bucket brigade drew water from the ship's starboard side, carried it to the engine room, and simulated throwing it on the "fire." Another crew carried the buckets to the main deck and threw the water over the port side. But when orders became confused in translation, the bucket brigade started to draw the water from the starboard side, run over to the port side, and then throw the water overboard, bypassing the engine room completely.

A 1960s stunt was for a carload of teenagers of college students to stop at a red light, whereupon at the command "Chinese fire drill," driver and passengers got out, ran around the car, and returned to their original seats.

The same idea is sometimes heard as the equally politically incorrect "Chinese square dance."

circle the wagons!: prepare your defenses.

A line in Western movies, when the Indians were about to attack a wagon train, was the wagon master's shout to "circle the wagons!" The Conestogas and prairie schooners then formed a circle to make a barricade behind which men fired their rifles at their attackers who galloped around the perimeter while the womenfolk reloaded the weapons or tended to the injured. (Another "oater" convention had the cavalry appear over the horizon and charge to the rescue).

You didn't have to wear a ten-gallon hat and carry a Winchester 73 to use the phrase. When trouble appeared, such as an advertising agency about to lose an important account, a "Mad Man" would summon his department with a "Let's get the wagons in a circle and save this sinking ship" (mixed metaphors were not unknown in the advertising business).

*

go fight city hall: the futility of challenging entrenched politicians or establishment.

Although sounding like a call to action, the phrase means that any effort to succeed against bureaucracy is doomed to failure. It was popularized, although not coined, in the book *Go Fight City Hall* by Ethel

Rosenberg, who with her husband Julius was later executed after being convicted of spying for Russia.

❦

clean as a hound's tooth: completely blemish-free or honest.

Another Southern expression; hounds' teeth are apparently cleaner than those of other species. Or perhaps just their canine teeth.

❦

Cloud Cuckoo Land: a nonexistent place of perfection, a utopia.

This phrase comes from *The Birds* by the Greek dramatist Aristophanes, in which the birds decide to build a perfect city called Cloud Cuckoo City. Over the years "City" became "Land."

❦

coals to Newcastle: Any unnecessary activity.

Before the days of railroading, goods and commodities were transported by water. Coal in particular was shipped to port city of Newcastle before being distributed to the rest of England. Therefore, unless you were the captain of a ship laden with coal, carrying that kind of fossil fuel to Newcastle was a waste of your time and energy.

cold comfort: offering limited sympathy or encouragement.

People who lost their jobs during the recession would likely take cold comfort from economic reports that an upturn was likely to occur in the future.

Shakespeare used the phrase in *King John*: "I do not ask you much, I beg cold comfort; and you are so strait / And so ingrateful, you deny me that."

❧

cold shoulder: intended indifference.

Although some sources contend that the phrase refers to serving unwanted or overstaying guests servings of the less preferable unheated leg of mutton, that's not where the expression came from. It first appeared in Sir Walter Scott's novel, *The Antiquary*, as a metaphor for disdain, the complete anthithesis of a warm hug.

❧

come and get it: the food is ready to be eaten.

This phrase most likely came from Western chuck wagon and logging camp cooks who fed platoons of hungry and rowdy cowboys and lumberjacks and who ruled their domain with an iron hand and skillet. The expression often ended with "before I throw it away."

The men didn't have to be told twice; anyone who arrived after the meal was served went hungry.

Many mothers used the phrase to summon their broods to the table, but with the decline of families eating dinner together, the phrase fell into disuse.

⁓

couldn't hit the side of a barn: a lousy shot.

This useful phrase can be applied to baseball pitchers who can't get the ball over the plate, basketball players who miss free throws, golfers whose balls routinely go out of bounds, target shooters and archers who miss the target, and anyone else who can't get it right.

Another similar farm-based expression is "couldn't hit a bull's ass with a barn shovel."

⁓

come a-cropper: to fail badly.

"Cropper" comes from a horse's croup or crupper, the part of the animal's back behind the saddle. Someone who parted company from his horse (an involuntary dismount, so to speak) was said to fall "neck and crop." That became "come a-cropper," first appearing in the foxhunting author Robert S. Surtees' 1858 novel *Ask Mamma*: [He] "rode at an impracticable fence, and got a cropper for his pains."

The phrase was picked up and applied to any misadventure, equestrian or otherwise.

꧁

cool your jets!: calm down!

This caution began with air force pilots reducing their jet planes' air speed and, by so doing, reducing strain on the engine caused by excess heat.

Among similar "relax!" phrases are "hold your horses!" "chill out!" "keep your pants on!" and "don't get your bowels in an uproar!"

꧁

conspicuous by its absence: very obvious through nonattendance.

This oxymoron, which goes back to ancient Rome, applies to people or objects that attracted attention because they were expected to be present but weren't. An example would be a close relative who either wasn't invited or chose not to attend a family function.

Some literary commentators contend that the phrase has become a cliché, but it's now used so rarely, you may—although at your peril—claim its wit to be your own.

꧁

country mile: a distance that's farther than anticipated.

Rural distances seem to be much longer than city folk think, so when a farmer says that the turnoff is "just a mile down the road," that mile can stretch on interminably.

The phrase used to be regularly used by baseball radio broadcasters to describe the distance of a long home run.

cricket on the hearth: A symbol of good luck and health.

A cricket on the hearth has been a sign of household luck for millennia and in many cultures. Crickets were widely considered to bring good fortune as well as a kind of companionship. Representations of a cricket have long been included as a fireplace decoration.

The expression "to find a cricket on the hearth is the luckiest thing of all" comes from Charles Dickens's novella, *Cricket on the Hearth*.

crocodile tears: false or hypocritical displays of emotions.

A 14th-century adventurer named Sir John Mandeville reported that crocodiles attract their prey's sympathy by weeping and then continued to cry while consuming their victims. Shakespeare referred to such a belief in Othello: "O devil, devil!

If that the earth could teem with woman's tears, /
Each drop she falls would prove a crocodile."

An alternate explanation is that since those reptiles
cannot cry, then crocodile tears are nonexistent shows
of emotion. However, and for what's it's worth, zoolo-
gists tell us that crocodiles do in fact have functional
tear ducts, although with no emotional connection.

༄

cry wolf: to raise a false alarm, to ask for assistance
when you don't need it, and by extension, to exaggerate or lie.

The phrase comes from the Aesop fable, "The Boy
Who Cried Wolf," in which a young shepherd found
it amusing to make villagers think a wolf is attacking
his flock. When they came to his rescue, they learned
of the false alarm. However, when a wolf actually men-
aced the flock, the villagers disregarded the shepherd's
calls for help, and the wolf ate the flock (and in some
versions the boy).

The moral: "Even when liars tell the truth, they
are never believed."

༄

crystal set: an early type of radio.

The first type of radio had only five components:
an antenna that picked up the signal, a wire tuning

coil with which the listener selected the station, an earphone to hear the broadcast, a ground wire to dissipate the electricity, and at the heart of the apparatus, a crystal detector that produced the audible signal. The crystal was a tiny chip of crystalline ore or stone such as galena.

Generations of youths built the sets from scratch and spent hours hunched over the device to hear broadcasts from nearby stations.

The reception range tended to be limited, so the introduction of diode tubes that increased reception marked the end of crystal sets' popularity.

‹ᴓᴏ

my cup runneth over: blessed with an overwhelming quantity of good things.

The phrase comes from the twenty-third Psalm that begins "The Lord is my shepherd": "Thou annointest my head with oil; My cup runneth over."

This expression of an image of an overflowing bounty was once far more prevalent than it now is, primarily because there's now far less familiarity with the Bible.

‹ᴓᴏ

curry favor: to ingratiate oneself through flattery or a willingness to please.

"Curry" has nothing to do with the spice—it means to groom, as in the horse-keeping currycomb tool. One of the definitions of "stroke" is "suck up to," and the image is similar—to get on a person's good side, whether or not flattery is warranted.

"Favor" was originally "Fauvel," the donkey who was the rogue hero of a 14th-century French romance. The image of grooming the beast to get on its good side or to win its favor is now the modern use of the word in the phrase.

᛫ ᚱᚢ

curtain lecture: a reprimand that a wife gives her husband.

"Curtain" refers to the drapery on canopied beds; the image is that of a wife giving hubby a piece of her mind in the privacy of their bedroom.

᛫ ᚱᚢ

cut in: ask the woman of a dancing couple to dance.

Youngsters in this age of couples spending an entire evening dancing only with each other would be surprised to learn that there was a time when they didn't (ask your parents or grandparents). One separation came from the practice of cutting in: an unattached male approached a couple on the dance floor, tapped the man on the shoulder, and asked "Do you mind if I cut in?"

Convention required that the male dancer graciously relinquish his place, although if he or the woman would prefer to continue together or the woman didn't want to dance with a certifiable nerd, one or the other might say something like "Thank you, but we're in the middle of a serious conversation." That was not a valid excuse, however, if the band was playing a jitterbug.

૮≈ઇ

D

dance card: a list of dance partners.

Although the youth of today may find it hard to believe, there was a time when couples that went to a party or a dance danced with other people.

This was especially true at proms, cotillions, and balls. In order for a woman, and not just the belle of the ball, to keep track of her partners, she entered their names on a dance card, a small booklet issued by the event's organizers that was attached to the wrist or dress with a thin cord. It was then up to the gentlemen to remember their partners for the evening (men often kept their own lists).

As a marginally polite but pointed way to brush someone off, you might smile and say, "I'd love to, but my dance card is filled."

dander up: to be angry.

"Dander" is the particles of hair that break off an animal's hair (humans call it "dandruff" when it happens to us). "To get your dander up" calls to mind the hair that stands up on the nape of an enraged dog's neck.

Another meaning of the word is the ferment used in making molasses; getting your dander up in that context suggests that your anger is rising the way yeast or any other leavening or fermenting agent does.

Darby and Joan: a devoted elderly couple leading an uneventful life.

These paradigms of lengthy connubial bliss first appeared in an 1735 poem by the otherwise-forgotten Henry Woodfall; the Darby in question was the master to whom Woodfall had been a printer's apprentice.

More distinguished authors who referred to the couple included Lord Byron, William Makepeace Thackeray, Anthony Trollope, Robert Louis Stevenson, and Henry James.

And they also appear in Jerome Kern and Oscar Hammerstein II's wistful ballad, *The Folks Who Live on the Hill* ballad: "We'll sit and look at the same old view / Just we two / Darby and Joan who used to be Jack and Jill . . ."

daylight robbery: an outrageously high price.

An appliance store advertises a refrigerators for $900, but you see ads for the same brand and model elsewhere for half that price. That store, you conclude, is committing highway robbery, a "crime" so metaphorically blatant that it is being committed in broad daylight.

That's not to be confused with "highway robbery." "Daylight robbery" offers you the option of paying the money or not, but you don't have that choice in "highway robbery," just as the victim of a stagecoach holdup had no choice. Your city raises property taxes. You receive the bill, take one look, and scream, "That's highway robbery!"

days of yore: time past.

"Days of yore" is an archaic phrase once used in historical narratives (e.g., describing tales of King Arthur and his Round Table) and now heard only – and very rarely—in a humorous context. "Yore" comes from the Middle English word for "year," which echoes its archaism.

as dead as a doornail: really dead.

Doornails, which provided strength and decoration, were hammered into the wood and then clenched for additional grip. Because a doornail was bent, it could not be used again, which made it even deader.

A more recent phrase is "as dead as last year's tennis balls." In the era before year-round indoor tennis, they would have lost their bounce before the start of the next season.

❧

Dead Man's Hand: a symbol of bad luck.

The cards in question were two aces and two eights, all four in the two black suits, that Wild West hero James Butler "Wild Bill" Hickcock reported held in the fatal poker game when he was shot in the back of the head by Jack McCall on August 2, 1876, at Deadwood, South Dakota. History does not reveal what the fifth "kicker" card was, although legend has it as the five, nine, or jack of diamonds.

❧

death and taxes: symbols of inevitability.

Benjamin Franklin observed that "In this world nothing can be said to be certain, except death and taxes." English novelist Daniel Defoe said much the same thing a century earlier.

❧

Deo volente (abbreviated to D.V.): God willing.

People who wanted to display the piety and knowledge of Latin, the latter more often than the former, used the phrase the way we now use "hopefully."

❧

derring do: heroically brave exploits.

"Derring" comes from "daring, and "do" is related to "done." Geoffrey Chaucer originated the phrase in his poem *Troilus and Criseyde*, it was picked up by Edmund Spenser and again by Sir Walter Scott in *Ivanhoe*. If you come across it in contemporary speed or writing, you're more than likely to hear it in the longer phrase "deeds of derring do."

❧

diamond in the rough: a basically admirable person who is full of potential, but lacks the social graces.

The image is that of a raw gemstone that, once cut and polished, will shine.

❧

the die is cast: no turning back; past the point of no return.

In 49 BC, Julius Caesar led his troops across the Rubicon, a river in northern Italy, in violation of Roman law. As he acted on his decision, he was said to have reflected, *Alea iacta est* (also *alea jacta est)*, Latin: for "the die has been cast." He referred to the singular of dice, proving that life was a crap shoot even back then.

❧

"Doctor Livingstone, I presume?"

A 19th-century explorer named Dr. David Livingstone became something of a national hero through his articles and lectures about his adventures in Africa. In 1864, Livingstone led an expedition to discover the source of the Nile. When little to nothing was heard from or about Livingstone after many years, Europeans and Americans became concerned. In 1871, the publisher of the *New York Herald* hired Henry Stanley, a newspaper reporter, to find Livingstone. Heading a group of some two hundred men, Stanley headed into the African interior. After nearly eight months he found Livingstone in a small village on the shore of Lake Tanganyika.

As Stanley described the encounter, "As I advanced slowly toward him I noticed he was pale, looked wearied . . . I would have embraced him, only, he being an Englishman, I did not know how he would receive me; so I . . .walked deliberately to him, took off my hat, and said, 'Dr. Livingstone, I presume?'

The phrase "'Dr. Livingstone, I presume?" caught the public's fancy, and any number of would-be wits greeted friends with it until the phrase lost all traces of cleverness. But that never stopped people from continuing to use it long past the public's memory of who Livingstone or Stanley were.

⌀

dollars to doughnuts: stakes for a bet on a certain outcome.

In the days when a dollar was worth more than it is now and a doughnut cost considerably less, someone who was reasonably sure that an event would happen might preface his comment with "Dollars to doughnuts . . ." as in "Dollars to doughnuts, it'll rain before nightfall."

⌀

drop a dime: to snitch, to betray.

Once upon a time, pay phones in enclosed booths could be found on most urban streets as well as in other public areas. Vandalism was rare, so the phones worked, and equally surprising to us today, local calls cost a dime.

A person who wanted to report something to the authorities that he or she didn't want anyone to overhear and didn't want the call traced located a secluded phone booth and deposited ten cents. That's the dime that was dropped down the coin slot.

The dime-dropper took a big chance, because if the droppee found out, the rat stood a good chance of being exterminated.

❧

get off the dime: to move or to stop wasting time.

Back in the 1920s and '30s, taxi dancers were female dance hall employees whose livelihood was dancing with any men who paid for the opportunity. The usual fee was ten cents, but that's not what "dime" in "get off the dime" meant.

Dancing with man after man for hours on end was tiring business, and the women often draped themselves over their partners and moved their feet as little as possible, no more than the width of a dime.

Although the men didn't object, dance hall managers did. That sort of mobility might lead to hanky-panky that would invite attention from the police and other enforcers of public morality. "Get off the dime" was the order, whereupon the women were then obliged to take more energetic dance steps.

Some Other "Dog" Phrases

Every dog will have its day: Everyone will have a moment of glory or the chance for revenge.

Andy Warhol's prediction that everyone will have fifteen minutes of fame was the most recent incarnation of this old expression, which has been traced back to the medieval Dutch scholar and theologian Desiderius Erasmus. According to Erasmus, the Greek playwright Euripides was killed by a pack of dogs that a rival set upon him.

Shakespeare picked up on the expression in Hamlet: "Let Hercules himself do what he may / The cat will mew and dog will have his day."

You can't teach an old dog new tricks: Getting people to change their habits or acquire new skills is impossible.

Puppies are teachable, but older dogs are less apt to be able to be trained, or so popular wisdom had it. By the same token, an octogenarian who has read the morning newspaper for decades is unlikely to be willing, much less eager, to switch to the online edition.

A barking dog never bites: making threats but not carrying them out.

The idea that a dog that vocalizes disapproval will not attack is more poetry than truth, as an examination of any hospital emergency room records will show.

This anecdote is relevant: a candidate for local political office went from door to door to solicit votes. Ringing a doorbell, he was greeted by a woman restraining a large dog that was barking loudly. When the candidate hesitated, his assistant encouraged him to stay, saying, "Don't you know the proverb 'a barking dog never bites'?"

"Yes," said the candidate, "I know the proverb, and you know the proverb, but does the dog know the proverb?"

(Barking dogs figure in another phrase: "My dogs are barking" means that my feet hurt.)

Why keep a dog and bark yourself?: Don't do a chore that should be done by someone you hired to do it.

A literal example of the expression would be a home owner who buys, trains, and maintains a guard dog, but stays up all night in case of intruders.

Jonathan Swift in *Polite Conversation* wrote this exchange between a woman of quality and her servant: "'Good Miss, stir the Fire.' 'Indeed your Ladyship could have stirr'd it much better.' [to which the woman replied] 'I won't keep a Dog and bark myself.'"

three dog night: a very cold night.

Back in pre-central heating days, on nights when a thick quilt wasn't available or didn't provide enough heat, rural dwellers might take a dog into bed to provide additional warmth. Chilly weather called for one dog, even colder for two, but when it was cold enough to freeze a brass monkey, you'd make room for three dogs.

"well, dog my cats": an expression of astonishment.

"Dog" may have been euphemism for "damned," as in "I'll be doggone." "Cats" might have been just something opposed to "dog."

The earliest written reference is in O. Henry's 1910 short story, *Memoirs of a Yellow Dog*: "I began to feel sorry for Hubby, dog my cats if I didn't."

dog in the manger: not permitting others to enjoy something you don't need out of spite, a spoilsport.

In Aesop's fable of the same name, a dog took a nap in a manger full of hay. When an ox entered and tried to get to its feed, the dog barked menacingly and refused admission, even though the hay was of no value to the dog. The moral: "People often grudge others what they cannot enjoy themselves."

❧

Don't take any wooden nickels: Don't let yourself be cheated.

This expression was first heard in the early 20th century. Although there never were any wooden nickels as legal tender, country folk going to a city were likely to be cheated by all manner of ruses, including obviously counterfeit coins.

Wooden nickels did exist, however, as bank promotions during and after the Great Depression; the "coins" were redeemable for prizes.

❧

Dorian Gray: someone who never appears to age.

In his novel, *The Picture of Dorian Gray*, Oscar Wilde told the story of the title character who made a Faustian arrangement with an artist to paint his portrait, the proviso being that Gray would not age, but the face in his painting would. As with such pacts, Gray lived to rue it.

It didn't take long before "Dorian Gray" was applied to anyone who showed no signs of aging. If, for example, after ten or twenty years you met a long-lost friend who looked much the same as when you last saw him or her, you would acknowledge that miracle as "Hey, it's Dorian Gray." And if your friend recognized the allusion, the reply was likely to be, "Yeah, but you should see the painting in my attic."

⌀

double feature: two movies for the price of one.

Movie theater owners during the Great Depression of the 1930s hit on the idea of attracting more business during those troubled times by offering not one but two feature-length films. That was in addition to the newsreels, cartoons, serial episodes, coming-attraction trailers, and short subjects that moviegoers had grown accustomed to seeing.

The two films were not of equal quality. One was the feature, the star-studded movie that people wanted to see. The second feature was a B movie.

Double features lasted through World War II up to the 1960s, when the studios insisting that theaters rent two films at a time was declared illegal.

down on his uppers: needy; fallen on hard times.

Men's shoes have two parts: the bottoms (soles and heels) and the uppers, which cover the foot. Someone whose financial condition was so bad that he couldn't afford to have the soles and heels replaced after being worn away was literally down on (in the sense of "to") his uppers.

A similar phrase is "down at the heels," and moving higher, "out at the elbows."

⟨᎘⟩

got the dragon: having bad breath.

Hear the monster bellow, and if you're close enough to smell what's coming out of its mouth, you'll have the picture.

⟨᎘⟩

dressed to the nines: wearing fashionably elegant clothing.

History fails to offer a definitive explanation for this phrase. Among those that have been advanced are emulating the Nine Worthies of the ancient world, the British Army's 99th Foot Regiment's smart uniform, the nine buttons on a medieval woman's gloves, and the nine muses. Whatever the real derivation, we can agree that "nine" has a special significance in the English language, as in "cloud nine" and "the whole nine yards."

❧

droit de seigneur: the supposed right of a nobleman to deflower the bride of any of his serfs on their wedding night. The phrase, which translates as "the lord's right" was also known as "the law / right of the first night."

Despite its widespread appearance in popular culture, reports of the "right" having been exercised are very rare. It was more a representation for or a warning about the power that a feudal lord could exert over his tenants.

Mozart's opera, *The Marriage of Figaro*, involves Count Almaviva's efforts to exercise his right with Figaro's bride, Susanna.

The phrase survives as a seldom-used metaphor for unlimited authority over another, such as a boss over an employee, notwithstanding the gender of either party.

❧

drugstore cowboy: a derisive phrase for a fashionably dressed man who loitered around public places trying to pick up women.

The phrase, which may have originated with movie cowboys who wore their costumes when they broke for lunch, brings to mind the fashion plate's inability to ride anything more challenging than a drugstore counter stool.

❧

drunk as a lord: extreme drunk.

Members of the nobility could afford to keep quantities of wine, beer, and liquor on hand, and as much out of envy as stating a fact, the common folk described anyone, titled or not, who had a load on by that phrase.

In these more egalitarian times, "drunk as a skunk" and, less elegantly, "shit-faced drunk" have replaced "drunk as a lord."

❧

like a drunken sailor: with no restraint.

A merchant seaman on shore leave with months' worth of pay in his pocket tended to make up for lost time in the drinking and "play-for-pay romance" departments. Fiscal restraint was out of the question. So did miners and cowboys when they too had a chance to go to town, but the image of a sailor prevailed.

The sea shanty "What Shall We Do with the Drunken Sailor?" suggests the same idea of a jocular attitude toward an inebriated mariner.

∽

duck soup: easy to accomplish.

The first appearance of the phrase was in a 1902 newspaper cartoon that had nothing to do with ducks. Not then and not now has anybody been able to suggest a likely derivation. If you're interested in an expression that makes sense, try the equivalent, "as easy as falling off a log."

∽

duck and cover: seek shelter.

If you attended elementary or secondary school during the 1950s and '60s, you will remember air raid drills practiced in the anticipation of nuclear attack. At the teacher's command "duck and cover," you would stop whatever you were doing, drop down under your desk or against a wall, and assuming a fetal position, interlace the fingers of both hands behind your neck in a "covering" pose.

How effective the technique would have been would have depended how far away from the atomic or hydrogen bomb blast's heat, shock waves, and radiation the school was. In any event, defense authorities thought everyone should do something in case of a nuclear attack. In those days, schoolkids did what they were told, so they ducked and covered.

❧

"Put up your dukes!": a challenge to fight.

The "dukes" in question were fists, which the challenged party was asked to clench in preparation to trying to punch his opponent. But why "dukes?" The word comes from Cockney rhyming slang "Duke of York," meaning "fork," held at mealtimes by a clenched fist.

Similarly, "duke it out" remains a general term for fighting.

❧

dumb Dora: a dimwit female.

The phrase was popularized by George Burns and Gracie Allen's vaudeville act in which Gracie played the hysterically illogical character that she later made famous under her own name during the pair's radio and television career.

Chic Young, better known for his *Blondie* comic strip, illustrated a foolish flapper named Dumb Dora. The cartoon lasted under several other illustrators from 1924 till 1935, well before "dumb blonde" became all the rage.

❧

durance vile: a lengthy prison sentence.

"Durance" meant "duration," and "vile" has its contemporary meaning of loathsome. That pretty well described long-term incarceration from the Middle Ages down to much of today's world.

ॐ

dunce cap: the mark of ignorance.

Before more enlightened pedagogical theories came into practice, students who were considered slow learners or even completely incapable of learning were made to sit on a high stool in a classroom corner while wearing a tall, conical paper cap with the word "dunce" on it. The rationale was that such embarrassment would encourage the child to try harder and do better (perhaps as a traumatized juvenile delinquent).

Such headgear has gone the way of the three Rs taught to the tune of a hickory stick, but as a phrase, people who make a mistake then smack themselves up the side of the head while uttering a Homer Simon–like "doh!" might then ask rhetorically "Where'd I leave that dunce cap?"

"Dunce" has an interesting derivation. It comes from the medieval philosopher John Duns Scotius, whose ideas were considered foolish. He and his followers wore conical hats, the top meant to point toward higher wisdom. The similarity to dunce caps is inescapable.

Dutch courage: bravery acquired by drinking alcohol.
Political and economic rivals during the 17th century, England and Holland fought a series of wars. English propagandists spread the rumor that Dutch soldiers and sailors developed the necessary nerve to fight only after drinking gin and other alcoholic beverages.

The Dutch haven't fared well in the English language. Other unflattering phrases are "Dutch treat (you pay for only yourself), "Dutch uncle" (a stern person, especially one who gave you a lecture you weren't happy about receiving), and "double Dutch" (gibberish).

E

egg on your face: to be embarrassed after being caught doing something wrong.

Among the possible origins are being red in the face about being told you left a smear of yolk around your mouth after breakfast or the humiliation that performers suffer when unhappy audiences pelt them with raw eggs. Closer to the mark is a barnyard explanation: farm dogs that develop the taste for raw eggs and break into the henhouse for a treat have that hang-dog look when confronted by their angry owners.

et tu, Brute? (pronounced "Bru-TAY"): an expression of feeling betrayed.

Marcus Brutus was one of the conspirators against Julius Caesar, formerly his great friend. Shakespeare's drama has Caesar's dying words the Latin for "and you, Brutus?" meaning "and you too" and uttered with tragic resignation as the Roman emperor recognized Brutus as one of his assassins.

⁓

"enclosed please find . . . ": formal business, writing for "it's in this envelope."

Until the middle of the 20th century, businesses corresponded in formal—some would say stilted—language. "Enclosed please find" was one phrase that, although still used by some law firms and insurance companies, is well on its way to join such archaisms as "in hand," ult. for "ultimo" (meaning "last month" as in "I have your letter of the 15th ult. in hand . . ."), inst. for "instant" or this month, and prox. for "proximo" or next month.

Perhaps e-mail abbreviations like LOL, IOW, and TTFN will someday be considered just as quaint.

⁓

cut one's eyeteeth: to have knowledge or skill gained through long experience.

"Eyeteeth" are the canines, which lie directly under our eyes. They cut through the gums when we were very young, so we've had them for almost as long as we've been alive. To ask a pianist how long she played ragtime might be answered with "Oh, I cut my eyeteeth on that kind of music." In other words, for a very long time.

Like many other childhood possessions, eyeteeth are so prized that "I'd give my eyeteeth" means to exchange a valuable asset for something that's highly desirable.

◈

F

fall off the cabbage truck: to be a naïve newcomer.

Imagine a flatbed farm wagon laden with fresh produce arriving in a city. Sliding off the back was a country bumpkin whose brain, or so smug sophisticated urbanites would agree, contained no more clue about worldly ways than a head of cabbage that might roll off the vehicle.

A similar expression was to say that someone "just got off the boat," a reference to immigration in the days of steamship passage when new arrivals were thoroughly ignorant of New World customs.

Among the snappy denials to being called a hick or greenhorn were "I wasn't born yesterday" or "I might have been born at night, but not <u>last</u> night" or the wonderfully imaginative Midwestern comeback, "Hey, what makes you think I just got off the noon balloon from Rangoon?"

⌘

fall on one's sword: to resign in a way to accept responsibility for a mistake.

In the era when warriors carried swords and shields, a soldier who was guilty of cowardice or another serious breach of military procedure was expected to do the "honorable thing" by taking his own life. He needed no assistance: he placed his sword's hilt on the ground and, resting the sharpened tip against his bare midsection, fell forward.

Although the accepted mode of remorse was a pistol bullet to the brain in the age of firearms, the phrase remained. It is now used metaphorically: a political figure or business executive whose resignation is an expression of regret for a badly made decision will be said to have fallen on his (or her) sword.

⌘

fast and loose: not straightforward or honest.

"Fast and Loose" was the medieval equivalent of the kind of con game now found in such scams as Three Card Monte. It involved two intricately arranged cloth straps. The victim was invited to choose one loop to place a stick through, and when the loop was pulled tight, the stick would be held fast and the victim would win a wager. However, the con artist had arranged both loops in such a way that either loop came free from the stick, no matter which one the victim selected, and the victim forfeited his bet. (Variations of the game under different names continue to this day.)

That's how the phrase "to play fast and loose," meaning dishonest, came to be used by people who never played the "game."

❧

a feather in your cap: an honor.

If you were praised or awarded a commendation, you had a feather in your cap. The phrase was most likely inspired by the idea that heroic Native American warriors were given additional plumage for their war bonnets.

❧

feeling one's Moxie: boundlessly energetic.

Moxie was a carbonated soft drink that began life at the end of the 19th century as a medicinal tonic (its inventor named it after a friend who supposedly discovered its key but unspecified ingredient). Thanks to an aggressive advertising campaign and key endorsements, Moxie became a nationwide success until World War II. It's now popular primarily in the New England area and Pennsylvania.

Gentian root gave Moxie its distinctive sharp flavor, which led to claims that it had energizing qualities. Hence the notion that someone who was feeling full of life was "feeling his Moxie."

Another peppy phrase comes from a breakfast cereal: "feeling your Wheaties."

❧

feet of clay: a flaw or vulnerability of someone who is otherwise admirable.

In the Bible's Book of Daniel, King Nebuchadnezzar dreamed that he saw a statue made of gold, silver, and brass, but with feet of clay. Daniel interpreted the vision to mean that the clay symbolized the Babylonian Empire's vulnerability and imminent collapse.

(see Achilles' heel.)

❧

fellow traveler: someone sympathetic to the beliefs and activities of an organization but not a member of that group.

The phrase originally applied to people in the early days of the Soviet Union who supported the Russian revolution and the Communist Party but were not members.

Communism was popular among many American intellectuals during the 1930s and '40s, but following World War II, this country's attitude toward the Soviets changed in light of Stalin's purges and revelations of espionage. Accusations that Soviet sympathizers had infiltrated our government and military led to congressional investigations, and the phrase "fellow traveler" was used to label those accused of "un-American" activities or even just "Communist dupes." Many such people found themselves blacklisted or otherwise persecuted.

A rarely used vestige of the phrase now applies to anyone who agrees with any viewpoint or faction but does not publicly work for it.

The Soviet Union named its early space satellites "Sputnik," the Russian word for "fellow traveler."

⌘

Fibber McGee's closet: a mess.

The *Fibber McGee and Molly* radio show chronicled the title characters' lives through the Depression and beyond (the show ran from 1935 to 1959).

The gentle family-friendly humor came from Fibber McGee's hatching far-fetched get-rich schemes that never materialized, not to the surprise of his long-suffering but supportive wife Molly.

The McGees's house was noted for its overstuffed closet. Audiences eagerly awaited someone, usually Fibber himself, to open its door, whereupon the sound of a landslide of glassware and other breakables filled the airwaves. The noise went on for what seemed an eternity, followed by a brief moment of silence, and then the sound of one final item (portrayed by one chime of a hand bell) and McGee's resolution to straighten the closet "one of these days."

"Fibber McGee's closet" entered the language as a metaphor for any example of domestic disarray, especially in a basement, attic, or—of course—a closet.

რომ

fiddler's bidding: last-minute invitation.

The image is a vacancy at a dinner table to which an itinerant fiddler who appeared at the door and asked to play for food was invited to join the household at the table.

რომ

fire extinguisher: a chaperone.

This 1920s phrase referred to a chaperone, whose presence and vigilance prevented romantic sparks from bursting into flames of passion.

რომ

fish or cut bait: do it or leave.

The entire expression was "fish or cut bait or go ashore," a commercial fishing industry warning that if you weren't hauling in a catch, you'd better find something more useful to do, such as cutting baitfish into pieces. And if you couldn't do that, you were just taking up space and you'd be fired.

A similar expression that's still in use is the non-gender specific "pee or get off the pot" (or in slightly less genteel surroundings, "shit or get off the pot").

෴

neither fish nor fowl: having no specific characteristics or category, not easily characterized.

The phrase, which was originally "neither fish nor flesh nor fowl," appeared in slightly different form in a 16th-century collection of proverbs as "neither fish, nor flesh, nor good red herring": fish for monks who ate no meat, flesh for people who could afford meat, and cheap herring for the poor.

The phrase is reminiscent of the old riddle: What is neither fish nor flesh, feathers nor bone/but still has fingers and thumbs of its own? Answer: a glove.

෴

better fish to fry: more important things to do.

This way of saying that you don't want to waste your time with something (or someone) goes back to 17th-century England. Its French equivalent is "other dogs to whip." Variations are "other fish to fry" and "better fish to fry."

⌘

fit to be tied: very angry and upset.

The image is being so agitated that only by being physically restrained, as if in a straightjacket, would a person be prevented from doing something rash and regrettable.

⌘

flash in the pan: an ultimate disappointment after a promising start.

Flintlock muskets and pistols had a priming pan that was filled with a small quality of gunpowder. When the trigger was pulled, the flint struck a piece of steel to create a spark that ignited the powder, which in turn set off the main gunpowder charge to launch the musket ball.

Whenever the flint-and-steel spark failed to light the main charge, there was a flash in the pan, but no shot. And that was the disappointment after a potentially useful beginning.

⌘

flea in his ear: a sharp, unwelcome rebuke.

To have a flea literally inserted in your ear would be an unwanted nuisance, just as being scolded, even if deserved, would be.

The British use the phrase to mean "put a bug in the ear": to plant a suspicion. The French "put a flea in the ear" to arouse amatory feelings, hardly an aphrodisiacal image (any more than a Spanish fly would be).

⌘

flimflam artist: a swindler.

Flimflam artist indulged in confidence games in which the victim is persuaded to buy worthless property. These crooks go after bigger game than street hustlers, card sharps, or bait and switchers do because of the time and preparation that their scams require.

"Flimflam" has been traced back to a Scandinavian word, although folk etymology has come up with a connection to an early 20th-century New York City law firm of dubious reputation, Flam & Flam.

⌘

flip side: the other side of a 45 or 78 rpm vinyl record.

The phrase was popularized by radio disc jockeys in the context of ". . . and that was Chuck Berry singing his latest hit, *Roll Over Beethoven*—and now let's hear the flip side, *Drifting Heart*."

When a song became a hit, its side of the record became the "A side" and the flip side was then referred to as the "B side." Then CDs made As and Bs passé.

⳩

flushed down the tubes: defeated.

A 1950s college expression drawn from waste removal. After an exam that was more difficult than anticipated, a student might groan, "Man, did I get flushed down the tubes!"

⳩

fly in the ointment: a spoiler.

Ecclesiastes 10:1 relates that dead flies impart a bad odor to perfume; early versions translate the word "perfume" as "ointment." Another old phrase with the same meaning is to "throw a monkey wrench in the works."

⳩

fly off the handle: to lose one's temper.

The image is one of speed, as rapidly as an axe head parting company from the handle during a down stroke. The phrase is credited to the 19th-century humorist Thomas Haliburton.

⳩

fold like a cheap suitcase: collapse easily.

Expensive luggage was made, as now, from well-constructed leather or fabric. Cheap ones used to be made of cardboard with little or no structural reinforcement, not very sturdy especially when manhandled by baggage handlers or hotel porters. A sports team with no defense or a poker player with a losing hand would both fold like a cheap suitcase.

You'd also hear "fold like a cheap suit," but since fabric folds easily, whether it's cashmere or polyester, "suitcase" presents a better connotation of a losing proposition.

の

footloose and fancy free: unattached, especially romantically, and able to move and act without responsibilities.

The "foot" is the bottom of a sail, and a sail that is footloose is free to move whichever way the wind blows. So is a person who is "footloose and fancy free," at liberty to follow any and all whims. (Such a state sounds enviable, but keep in mind the fable about "The Grasshopper and the Ant.")

の

Forty acres and a mule: a government handout; a broken promise.

As Union general William T. Sherman marched through Georgia and other parts of the confederacy during the Civil War, he promised freed slaves the gift of forty acres of South Carolina and Georgia farmland and an army mule with which to work the soil. Following the war, however, President Johnson rescinded Sherman's order, and the appropriated land was restored to its owners.

While most citizens adopted the phrase as a metaphor for either any form of government handout (or a trifling salary or bonus from their employer), African-Americans who remembered the expression's history used it as a rueful reminder of a offer that was reneged upon.

❧

for want of a nail: a major catastrophe that can be traced back to a small error.

The lack of a basic part or a small object can lead from one unwanted consequence to another larger one to yet another one, as in a stack of falling dominos. The full proverb is "For want of a nail the shoe was lost. For want of a shoe the horse was lost. For want of a horse the rider was lost. For want of a rider the battle was lost. For want of a battle the kingdom was lost. And all for the want of a horseshoe nail."

❧

French leave: to leave without saying good-bye.

The British thought that sneaking away from a gathering without telling anyone you're going wasn't acceptable manners across the channel. Curiously, or perhaps typically, the French refer to the same practice as *filer à l'anglais* ("take English leave"). Americans used to use the phrase without knowing its origin.

It has been said that the French leave but never say good-bye, while Americans say good-bye but never leave.

"French leave" is also military slang for deserting.

❦

Frick and Frack (or "fric and frac"): two inseparable and indistinguishable companions.

Frick and Frack was a Swiss comedy ice skating duo who appeared in the original Ice Follies, starring in the late 1930s show as comedy ice skaters. Dressed in identical alpine lederhosen, they astonished audiences with extraordinary feats of athleticism.

Thereafter, any two guys who palled around together, especially if they were of the same build, were called "Frick and Frack." And since enough such pairs were considered cutups, "Frick and Frack" also came to mean two jokesters, the way a trio of town clowns was the Three Stooges.

four-flusher: a fraud, a bluffer.

To hold a four flush in poker is to have four cards of the same suit but not the fifth card that would make a potentially winning hand. Since four of a suit is worthless, a "four-flusher" is gambling that you'll believe her or she has the goods or the right stuff.

The suggestion that a four-flusher is so full of crap that getting all of it down the toilet will take four pulls of the handle is an imaginative but incorrect derivation of the phrase.

⁊

Fuller Brush man: a door-to-door salesman.

The Fuller Brush Company, founded in 1906, employed salesmen who went from house to house selling a variety of brushes, including a hairbrush that carried a lifetime guarantee. Among the company's accomplishments was making selling door-to-door an acceptable and profitable technique, one that was used (as long as local ordinances allowed) by sellers of encyclopedias, cosmetics, insurance, Girl Scout cookies, and other goods and services.

Through much of the first half of the 20th century, visitors would ring a friend's or neighbor's doorbell and then answer the query, "Who's there?" with "It's the Fuller Brush man!"

in the fullness of time: whenever appropriate or available.

Whereas we now fudge with "whenever it's ready" or "you'll have to wait," earlier generations answered questions with "in the fullness of time." For example, a politician's spokesman being asked, "When will the congressman comment on the allegations?" would have been counted on to counter, "In the fullness of time."

G

gag me with a spoon: a exclamation indicating disgust.

"Val-speak" was an idiom created in the 1970s by so-called Valley Girls, reputedly materialistic and self-centered young women who lived in California's San Fernando Valley (outside Los Angeles). Their vocabulary and speech patterns swept the country, propelled by popular music, television shows, and such movies as "Clueless" (based on Jane Austen's novel *Emma*).

Like other fads, linguistic or otherwise, Val-speak disappeared almost as quickly as it had burst on the scene. Where once the staple "gag me with a spoon" (meaning that something was awful enough to induce nausea), was widely heard, it's gone the way of "well, dog my cat" and other archaisms.

That's not to say that all Val-speak has disappeared. "As if" ("that's not going to happen"), "duh!" ("that's obvious"), and the ubiquitous "like" are heard wherever the English language is used . . . and misused.

✿

gift horse: something obtained at no charge, but not without an ultimate cost.

According to legend, it was Odysseus who devised the scheme of leaving a huge wooden horse in front of the gates of Troy, which the Greeks were unable to conquer (the losing side of a war traditionally left a gift for the victors). The Trojans watched the Greeks depart then dragged the horse inside their walls. Soldiers who had been hiding inside the horse surreptitiously opened the gates, the Greeks stole back inside the gates, and the rest is history.

The cautionary expression "beware Greeks bearing gift" is based on the legend, as is the phrase "gift horse." Stated another way, there ain't no free lunch.

✿

a gentleman and a scholar: a complimentary term for a person, especially one who has done you a favor.

Back in the era when courteous behavior and academic achievement were prized far more highly than they are today, acknowledging a kindness, such as holding the door or relinquishing a place on line so that someone else could get a taxi, would be met with a smile, a nod, and the phrase, "You are a scholar and a gentleman."

༙

get one's goat: to make angry.

Many racehorses develop a strong attachment to their stable mascots—dogs, cats, chickens, and, especially, goats. The mascots provide a calming effect—they're the horse's security blankets. One will live in or close to "its" horse's stall and will accompany the horse to racetracks across the country.

Horses become very upset when their mascots aren't around, so crafty stablehands would steal away a rival horse's pal. Thus deprived, the horse would become angry when someone got its goat.

༙

gild the lily: engage in an unnecessary and usually wasteful activity.

Like carrying coals to Newcastle, to gild a lily would be a waste of time as the flower already possesses more than sufficient beauty.

The phrase comes from a misquotation of lines from Shakespeare's *King John*:

Therefore, to be possess'd with double pomp,
To guard a title that was rich before,
To gild refined gold, to paint the lily . . .
Is wasteful and ridiculous excess.

❧

gloomy Gus: a perpetually unhappy person.

Gloomy Gus was a character in *Happy Houligan*, one of the earliest (1900) newspaper comic strips. Unlike his jovial brother Happy, saturnine Gus never smiled because he never found any reason to.

For much of the 20th century, pessimists and anyone else who happened to look sad was referred to as a "gloomy Gus."

❧

God's acre: a churchyard burial area.

The phrase is a translation of the German word, *Gottesacker*, "God's field" where the souls of the faithful are sown. The phrase also been used for the dedication of a portion of a farm field or a garden plot to growing food that will be given to the needy.

The phrase should not be confused with Erskine Caldwell's 1933 novel, *God's Little Acre*.

❧

go fly a kite: get lost!

Kite flying is an activity that is done far less now than in previous centuries. Accordingly, "go fly a kite!" is heard far less than "get lost!" "take a hike!" and "get your ass out of here!" (or something stronger).

go hog wild: become overly excited or enthusiastic.

Why the hog should have been singled out remains a mystery, unless porcine greediness was somehow connected with an overwhelming desire for excitement.

In any event, the phrase has now been overshadowed by "going ape-shit" (which raises even more intriguing simian speculation).

go to pot: become useless.

When a chicken or other edible farm animal outlived its earthly utility, it would be cooked and eaten. That's the pot to which it would go.

goody gumdrops: an expression of delight.

"Goody gumdrops" and "Goody, goody gumdrops" were popularized in Carl Ed's 1930s *Harold Teen* cartoon strip, although whether Ed originated the phrases is unclear.

"Gumdrops" referred to the candy, and the phrase's connotation was self-consciously cute, as if childish glee.

~∿~

goody two-shoes: a self-righteous, vain person.

The 18th-century children's story, *The History of Little Goody Two-Shoes*, attributed to Oliver Goldsmith, was a version of *Cinderella*. The title character, named after an already-established phrase, was an orphan who was so poor, she owned only one shoe. When a rich benefactor gave her a complete set of footwear, she repeated her delighted in having "two shoes."

The phrase "Goody Two-Shoes" developed its negative connotation because the girl subsequently married into money, which cast suspicion on her virtuous nature.

~∿~

good egg: an agreeable, helpful person.

The phrase applied to someone of value in terms of utility, the opposite of a no-good rotten egg. It was most often heard in such requests as "Be a good egg and mail this letter for me" or "Pour me another whisky, like a good egg."

~∿~

a good five-cent cigar: a sensibly affordable item.

The remark "What this country needs is a good five-cent cigar" was popularized by Thomas Riley Marshall, vice president of the United States under

Woodrow Wilson. In one account, he made the remark while presiding in the Senate after he heard a succession of senators enumerate what was lacking in the United States.

The remark, which most likely originated with a 19th-century humorist named Kin Hubbard, was appropriated by several generations of Americans to complain obliquely about overpriced items of any sort.

✤

good-time Charlie: an easygoing and sociable guy.

Popular in the 1920s, the phrase described a man who was always ready to have fun, although it sometimes meant someone who was your pal only during good times and who would desert you in your hour of need.

✤

the goose hangs high: everything is to your liking.

A plucked goose hanging in a larder is a sign that the family will have something to eat for the foreseeable future. But why is it hanging high? That may mean the bird is safe from rodents and other predators, or it could refer to something entirely different: a skein of flying geese fly close to the ground in bad weather, but high when conditions are good.

In either case, a goose hanging high is a good thing—except for the goose.

Gordian knot: a difficult problem that can be solved by an unexpected and simple method.

According to an old Greek legend, a poor peasant named Gordius appeared in the public square of Phrygia in an ox cart. Since an oracle had prophesized that the future king would ride into town in a wagon, Gordius was made ruler. In gratitude, Gordius dedicated his ox cart to Zeus and tied the cart to a pole with a highly intricate knot, whereupon an oracle foretold that whosoever untied the knot would rule all of Asia.

Although many tried in vain to untie the knot, it took Alexander the Great to do so, which he did with one cut of his sword. That might not have been the method that Gordius or the oracle had in mind, but it was good enough to enable Alexander to conquer most of Asia as well as a large chunk of the rest of the known world.

⸖

Great Unwashed: a disparaging term for the common man.

The phrase first appeared in an 1830 novel, *Paul Clifford*, by the British novelist and playwright Edward Bulwer-Lytton: "He is certainly a man who bathes and 'lives cleanly,' (two especial charges preferred against him by Messrs. the Great Unwashed)."

Among other cynics (although they would call themselves realists) who used the phrase was

H. L. Mencken, who also referred to the majority of Americans as the "booboisie."

⁂

grass widow: a woman temporarily or permanently separated from her husband.

Many times during and after the American West was settled, farmers decided that they had enough of such a bleak life, whereupon they left their wives and children. These abandoned women were known as grass widows, left out to grass on the Great Plains.

(The phrase is, however, much older. It was first used in 16th-century England to describe women of easy virtue who "slept" on beds of grass instead of mattresses and bed linen.)

"Grass widow" came to be applied to the wives of traveling salesmen, professional athletes, and other men who spent much of their year on the road. As that usage became obsolete, similar phrases appeared: golf widow, fishing or hunting widow, and any other sport that claimed their hubby's attention.

⁂

Greek to me: unintelligible, as in "I didn't understand a word he said—it was all Greek to me."

Shakespeare said it best in this exchange from *Julius Caesar.*

Cassius: Did Cicero say any thing?
Casca: Aye, he spoke Greek.
Cassius: To what effect?
Casca: Nay, an' I tell you that, I'll ne'er look you i' the face again: but those that understood him smiled at one another and shook their heads; but, for mine own part, it was Greek to me.

❧

Greeks bearing gifts: see "gift horse"

❧

Green Stamps: trading stamps.

The most popular of the trading stamps that shoppers collected from the end of the 19th century through the 1980s were S&H (Sperry & Hutchinson) Green Stamps. Supermarket chains, department stores, service stations, and other retailers bought the stamps, then gave them to shoppers in quantities and denominations based on how much the shoppers spent in the store. The object was to create customer loyalty. Shoppers then cashed in the stamps at redemption centers or by mail and received household and sporting goods as well as other items.

"Do you give Green Stamps?" was a frequent question, and not always to retailers. A would-be wit might ask a dinner party hostess serving a platter of

❧

food, "Do I get Green Stamps with that?" Said often enough, it was enough to make the rest of the gathering lose their appetites.

‿

H

hair of the dog that bit you: more alcohol to counteract the effects of a hangover.

Most ancient civilizations and many modern ones believed that the most effective cure for a dog bite was a bundle of the canine's hair tied inside or around the wound. On the same theory that the injury's cause could also be the cure came the metaphor for taking a drink of alcohol to lessen, if not eliminate, the discomfort of "the morning after."

There's some truth to the idea: a Bloody Mary, Screwdriver, and another alcoholic beverage will take the edge off your hangover by making you drunk (or drunker) again, but alas, another slug of the demon rum won't cure the underlying problem, and at some point the piper will have to be paid.

‿

hair shirt: a self-imposed act of atonement.

The wearing of shirts made of unprocessed animal hair or a rough cloth next to the skin dates back to biblical days. The purpose of such an uncomfortable garment was as an expression of faith, a constant reminder that the wearer's sinful flesh was inconsequential compared to a commitment to God. Some members of the nobility wore hair shirts to compensate for the luxury with which they surrounded themselves.

Although such mortification of the flesh is rare these days, "hair shirt" survives as a metaphor for self-imposed penitence. A basketball player who takes cold showers for the next month as penance after missing what would have been a game-winning shot has chosen to wear, as it were, a liquid hair shirt.

⚬

half-cocked: prematurely.

Like "flash in the pan," "half-cocked" is a phrase that comes from old firearms. The firing mechanism of a flintlock pistol or musket could be set at full cock, or ready to be discharged, or half cock, which was the equivalent of having a safety on a revolver. A weapon that went off while half-cocked did so prematurely, just like someone who loses his temper without considering the facts or consequences of a situation. To act too soon, especially in a rash or impetuous fashion, is to go off half-cocked.

⚬

hand over fist: continuously.

A sailor hauls in lines ("ropes" to you, landlubbers) not by jerky interrupted pulls, but in a smooth hand-over-hand motion. That's the image applied to people who make money hand over fist, which is how the phrase is most always used.

❧

handwriting on the wall: a dire warning.

The phrase comes from the Book of Daniel, in which the Persian king Belshazaar and his court see a disembodied hand appear during a feast and write on a wall, "*Mene, Mene, Tekel u-Pharsin.*"

His seers unable to decipher the words, the king summons Daniel, who, keeping his interpretation streak intact: [see "feet of clay"], reveals that the words refer to Belshazaar's reign and his kingdom being in jeopardy. And sure enough, later that evening the king was murdered and his kingdom given to the Medes, just as Daniel had predicted.

"The handwriting on the wall" or "the writing on the wall" came to refer to any prediction or omen that a venture was doomed to failure.

❧

the Hatfields and the McCoys: a long-lasting and bloody feud.

The Hatfields and the McCoys were two warring families who lived along the West Virginia-Kentucky border. The 1865 murder of a McCoy, a returning Union soldier, allegedly by a band of Confederate sympathizers was attributed to a member of the Hatfield family. The death sparked some thirty years of hatred and much bloodshed between the two clans, a situation that was hardly improved when a McCoy woman ran off to live with a Hatfield who ultimately abandoned her.

As word of the lengthy feud spread across the country and for years after it was settled, the two sides became a metaphor for neighborly bad blood. When, for example, two families stopped talking when one chopped down a tree on the property line between them, others in the neighborhood were likely to refer to the situation as "the Hatfields and the McCoys going at it."

❧

happy as a duck in Arizona: unhappy.

Ducks like water. Arizona is a largely arid state. Ergo, an unhappy person would be as unhappy as a teal in Tucson.

Contrast that condition with someone who is as happy as a clam at high tide or as a flea in a doghouse.

❧

halcyon days: a calm and peaceful period of time.

There was an old belief that two weeks of calm weather were to be expected just before and after the winter solstice, when the halcyon bird (a species akin to the kingfisher) calmed the sea in order to lay and hatch her eggs on a floating nest. That idea originated with the Greek myth of Alcyone, daughter of Aeolus, god of the winds, who was married to the king of Thessaly. When the king was drowned at sea, Alcyone threw herself into the water in her grief. However, the gods transformed her into the halcyon bird whom the wind carried to be reunited with her husband.

෨

heaping Pelion upon Ossa. adding difficulty to difficulty; fruitless efforts.

The reference is to the attempt by the giants in Greek mythology to climb to heaven by piling Mount Ossa upon Mount Pelion.

෨

since Hector was a pup: a very long time ago.

One explanation suggests that the expression might have become popular in the 1920s when many schoolboys studied Greek and had dogs named Hector after the Homeric hero. Another possibility is also rooted in classical studies: according to the playwright Euripides, Hector's mother, Hecuba, was turned into a dog for murdering the killer of her older son; therefore, Hector was the son of a dog, which made him a pup.

In any event, the phrase is now obsolete.

⌘

heebie-jeebies: anxiety or fear.

Records indicate that "heebie-Jeebies" first appeared in print in a 1923 newspaper cartoon by one Billy DeBeck, in which a character says, "You dumb ox—why don't you get that stupid look offa your pan—you gimme the heeby jeebys!"

The spelling changed over the years, as witnessed by its inclusion a year later in the "Alabamy Bound" popularized by the Paul Whitman Orchestra: "I'm Alabamy bound, there'll be no heebie-jeebies hanging 'round . . ."

⌘

go to hell in a handbasket [or handcart]: heading for trouble.

The expression might possibly have been inspired by the heads of decapitated prisoners falling or being dumped into handbaskets or handcarts. The "handbasket" alliteration following "going to hell"

caught on and was applied to anyone whose behav
ior was likely to lead to an unhappy consequence.

❧

hell-bent for leather: moving rapidly and with
determination.

"Hell" in this case strengthens the word "bent,"
which means a direct route (although it sounds as
though it should mean the opposite). "Leather"
refers either to a saddle or to a whip used to urge a
horse to move faster, or perhaps items.

"Hell for leather" meaning "all deliberate haste"
was a popular phrase in itself.

Among a number of variants is "hell-bent for election,"
said to have originated with the 1840 Maine gubernato-
rial race and appearing in an 1899 Stephen Crane story:
"One puncher racin' his cow-pony hell-bent-for-election
down Main Street." Others are "hell-bent for breakfast,"
"for Sunday," and "for Georgia."

❧

hem and haw: to refuse to give a definite answer.

"Hem," similar in derivation to the interjection
"ahem," meant to hesitate. "Haw" meant much the
same sense of being noncommittal. Combine the
two, and you have someone who's stalling for time
and hoping not to have to respond any further.

꩜

Hen-ree! Henry Aldrich! Coming, Mother!:
Henry Aldrich was a very popular radio show that
ran from 1939 to 1953. The title character was an
awkward adolescent who was forever getting into
hot water with his girlfriend and his other friends.

The show began with Mrs. Aldrich calling,
"Hen-ree, Henry Aldrich!" to which he would
reply, "Coming, Mother!" The phrase's elements
became 1940s catchwords for summoning and
responding, respectively.

꩜

hey, Rube!: a rallying cry for assistance when trouble
breaks out.

The phrase began in the days of touring carnivals and
circuses. A carnival or circus performer or stagehand
who found himself in an argument or altercation with
patrons or other outsiders yelled, "hey, Rube," the signal
for his colleagues to run and help him out.

An item in the *Chicago Tribune* in 1882 explained
that "a canvasman watching a tent is just like a man
watching his home. He'll fight in a minute if the
outsider cuts the canvas [to sneak in], and if a crowd
comes to quarrel—he will yell, 'Hey, Rube!' That's
the circus rallying cry, and look out for war when
you hear it."

"Rube" might have been the name of an actual person summoned for assistance, although another possibility is that "rube" referred, as it still does, to country
bumpkins; that is, to members of rural carnival and
circus audiences who were likely to start trouble.

આ

hide your light under a bushel: not to reveal hidden abilities.

The expression is usually used in advice to reveal
those talents and then use them. A bushel was a container for measuring grain. In Matthew 15:15, Jesus
said "Neither do men light a candle and put it under
a bushel but on a candlestick."

આ

high-button shoes: a symbol of times past.

Through the Victorian era up to the end of the first
World War, women wore ankle-high boots that fas-
tened with buttons. When the style lost favor with fashion, the footwear became of a symbol of a time gone by,
surving in the scornful expression that an old-fashioned
item or idea "went out with high button shoes."

Other such "went out with" objects were banjo
picks, horse collars, and buggy whips.

આ

highway robbery: see "daylight robbery."

❧

hill of beans: A negligible amount.

This phrase is most often heard as "that doesn't amount to a hill of beans." The underlying idea is that beans are so common that even a hill of them isn't worth very much, if anything at all.

The Yiddish word for "beans" is "bupkes," which has been adopted into American English to mean "absolutely nothing." You'll hear it at card games and racetracks when a disgusted player tosses in his hand or tears up a losing pari-mutuel ticket with an exasperated "I got bupkes."

❧

hitch your wagon to a star: set high goals.

The phrase come from an 1862 Ralph Waldo Emerson essay "American Civilization": "Now that is the wisdom of a man, in every instance of his labor, to hitch his wagon to a star, and see his chore done by the gods themselves. That is the way we are strong, by borrowing the might of the elements. The forces of steam, gravity, galvanism, light, magnets, wind, fire, serve us day by day, and cost us nothing."

It used to be heard among other bit of avuncular or graduation speech advice.

Then advice for the future became more specific, like "plastics" in the movie *The Graduate*. Nowadays, in this economy, your guess is as good as mine.

❧

hither and yon: near and far.

"Hither" means toward the speaker. "Yon" is "far away" (as in "beyond" and "over yonder"). Put them together and you've got all the territory covered.

Another similar archaic phrase is "hither and thither," meaning this way and that way, or a state of utter confusion.

❧

Hobson's choice: no choice at all, take it or leave it.

Thomas Hobson ran a livery stable in Cambridge, England in the 16th century. He had a simple policy about renting out his horses: you took what he gave you or you went horseless (some accounts say he rented whichever animal was in the stall nearest the door).

Hobson's spirit lives on in the joke about a passenger aboard El Al Airlines who asked the flight attendant what the choice of dinner was. She replied with a smile, "The choice is yes or no."

❧

hoist by your own petard: hurt by your own misdeed.

A petard was a medieval bomb made of a container of gunpowder with a fuse, and to blow open gates during sieges against towns and fortresses. Unreliable, petards often exploded prematurely and sent the person who lit the fuse aloft (the "hoist" image) in one or more pieces.

The phrase, which is often misquoted as "hoist <u>on</u> one's own petard," comes from *Hamlet*:

For 'tis the sport to have the engineer
Hoist with his own petard; and 't shall go hard
But I will delve one yard below their mines
And blow them at the moon . . .

❧

horizontal engineering: old college slang for taking a nap.

❧

the horse's mouth: the source of a truthful or honest statement.

A likely origin of the phrase is how a horse's age can be determined with a fair degree of accuracy by the number, length, and shape of its teeth. A seller might exaggerate an animal's age, but the merchandise's mouth would reveal the truth.

Hence the "straight dope" coming "right out of the horse's mouth."

᷈

a horse of another color: an entirely different matter.

In *Twelfth Night*, Shakespeare had a character say, "My purpose is, indeed, a horse of that colour," meaning "the very thing." It's not difficult to see how that phrase would be changed to "a horse of another color" to mean the opposite.

Other formerly popular equine expressions are "don't change horses in midstream" (stick to your original plan); "get off your high horse" (don't be so proud or smug); "don't beat a dead horse" (don't waste your time); "one-horse town" (a tiny rural community); and "horse show" (derisive college slang term for a debutante cotillion).

᷈

as hot as highway blacktop: scorching.

A typical summer day in the Deep South.

᷈

How now, brown cow?: a playful greeting.

The phrase began as a way for would-be actors and orators to develop round, "pear-shaped" vowels in their voice, the kind of "the rain in Spain . . ." elocution exercise that Professor Higgins had Eliza do in *My Fair Lady*.

The "how now?" salutation phrase became an open invitation to performers and nonperformers alike to greet friends with the entire expression. But that was then, and "whazzup?" and "what's happenin'?" is how it's now done.

⳹

hubba hubba: an expression of appreciation.

The phrase, along with the longer "hubba hubba ding ding" started during World War II, purportedly from a Chinese greeting "how-pu-how" that Air Force pilots learned from Chinese pilots trained at a Florida base. The phrase spread around the services, primarily due to comedian Bob Hope's radio broadcasts; Hope and sidekick Jerry Colonna used it frequently.

The phrase was expanded to "Hubba hubba ding ding / I see some-thing" whenever a pretty girl passed by. Or when a couple was spied chatting romantically, "Hubba hubba ding ding / Think about a wedding ring."

⳹

hue and cry: a loud public clamor

The phrase was most usually heard as "raise a hue and cry." According to old English law, any citizen who heard shouts that a possible lawbreaker was being pursued was required to join in the chase. The phrase is a combination of the Anglo-French *hu* (a shout of warning) and *cri* (to cry out).

⌐∞

humble abode: a self-deprecating way to refer to one's home.

Jane Austen's *Pride and Prejudice* is the source: the insufferable Mr. Collins refers to his patroness Lady Catherine de Burgh with "The garden in which stands my humble abode is separated only by a lane from Rosings Park, her ladyship's residence" and "But she is perfectly amiable, and often condescends to drive by my humble abode in her little phaeton and ponies."

⌐∞

humble pie: a meek admission of a mistake.

The "humble pie" that we eat when we make a misjudgment or outright error was originally "umble" pie made from the intestines of other less appetizing animal parts. Servants and other lower-class people ate them, as opposed to better cuts. "Umble" became "humble" over the years until eating that pie came to mean expressing a very meek *mea culpa*.

A similar phrase is "eat crow," the bird being as unpalatable a dish as one's own words.

⁓

hurly burly: a noisy confusion.

To hurl is to throw, and "hurly burly" is based on the image of a mob throwing things around chaotically.

The phrase appears in the opening scene of Shakespeare's *Macbeth* when the witches chant, "When shall we three meet again / In thunder, lightning, or in rain? / When the hurlyburly's done, / When the battle's lost and won."

⁓

I

"I gave at the office": an explanation for not contributing to a cause or organization, or an excuse not to donate or participate in anything.

Campaigns for civic and charitable causes like the Red Cross and Community Chest were once far more prevalent at places of business than they now are, and people routinely made donations. Someone who was approached at home or elsewhere could have a valid excuse of "I gave through the office."

By extension, the phrase came to be used to slough off any kind of request. For example, someone who asked for a $20 loan might have been met with "Sorry, I gave at the office."

An old chestnut of a joke tells about the man who was lost on a camping trip. Rescuers scoured the wilderness until a medical emergency team finally spotted a solitary figure across a wide chasm. "Charlie Smith," someone shouted," "is that you?"

"Yes, it is," came the reply. "Who are you?"

"We're from the Red Cross."

"I gave through the office!" Charlie shouted back.

༄

"If I knew you were coming, I'd have baked a cake": an expression of delighted surprise at finding someone whose appearance was unanticipated.

The title of a 1950 hit record by Eileen Barton, the phrase quickly caught on, and for at least a decade thereafter anyone who appeared where least expected was likely to be greeted with "If I knew you were coming, I'd have baked a cake."

༄

Indian giver: someone who gives a gift and then wants it returned.

Native Americans' economy was based on the barter system; therefore, an item that colonists and settlers took to be an outright gift was expected to be reciprocated. When it was not, the giver wanted the item returned.

The offensive phrase, which first appeared in mid-18th-century New England, is now rarely used . . . and properly so.

᷍

I'm from Missouri: Prove it!

Missouri's unofficial nickname is *the Show-Me State*, based on the inhabitants' reputed skepticism. One legend attributes the phrase's popularity to Congressman Willard Duncan Vandiver. While a member of the House Committee on Naval Affairs, he said at an 1899 naval banquet, "I come from a state that raises corn and cotton and cockleburs and Democrats, and frothy eloquence neither convinces nor satisfies me. I am from Missouri. You have got to show me."

Even people who didn't hail from that state could be heard to question something with "I'm from Missouri . . . you'll have to show me."

᷍

Include me out: I want no part of it.

Movie producer Samuel Goldwyn had as many malapropisms and other odd quotations attributed to him as Yogi Berra has, including "That oral contract isn't worth the paper it's printed on" and "Anybody who goes to a psychiatrist ought to have his head examined." One that caught on above and beyond the entertainment business was Goldwyn's "include me out" for any situation of which someone didn't want to be a part.

❧

"Information, please."
During the Dark Ages before computerized directory assistance, callers who didn't know a phone number dialed the operator and asked to be connected to "information." The information operator would then supply the number, and at no charge.

"Information" with "please" added in a more polite era, was adopted as the title of a very popular radio quiz show in which a panel of experts tried to answer questions submitted by listeners. The phrase then became widely used as a preamble to any sort of question.

The radio program was satirized by another quiz show whose title "It Pays to Be Ignorant" also became a brief fad in everyday speech.

❧

I shoulda stood in bed: I shouldn't have bothered.

This remark came from prizefight manager Joe Jacobs, who in 1935 saw his first baseball game, the opening game of the World Series between the Detroit Tigers and Chicago Cubs. It was a very cold day, and when asked what he thought of baseball, Jacobs replied, "I should have stood in bed."

The Cubs might have heeded that advice, because despite winning that opening game, they went on to lose the Series four games to two.

✑

It's the berries: superlative.

This 1920s phrase would seem to convey the idea that berries are a choice snack or dessert.

A similar phrase, "the bee's knees," has no such connection with reality aside from its rhyme and cute image.

✑

Ivy League: a preppy clothing style.

Named for the athletic federation of Columbia, Cornell, Dartmouth, Harvard, the University of Pennsylvania, Princeton, and Yale, "Ivy League" described a 1950s and '60s men's fashion: pants with no pleats and a buckle in the rear. The buckle could be used to expand or shorten the waist fit, although it was primarily for adornment. There were also British-influ-ence narrow-brim caps that had a buckle in the back.

Why "Ivy League"? The schools were considered (at least by some) to be sophisticated, elite, and thus worthy of emulation, an attitude that their students did little to disabuse.

࣪ৡ

J

jack of all trades: a versatile person.

"Jack" was commonly used as a synonym for "man," as in "every man jack," and the phrase was used in a highly complimentary way. But the addition of "and master of none" changed the expression to mean a dab-bler or dilettante, which wasn't very flattering at all.

࣪ৡ

jailhouse lawyer: a non-attorney who dispenses legal advice.

Properly speaking, a jailhouse lawyer is a prison inmate who, although not a law school graduate (much less a member of the bar), has the requisite skill to assist other prisoners with such legal matters as preparing and filing appeals, writs, and pardon requests. Much of such knowledge came from personal experience.

The phrase also applies to any layman, behind bars or not, who offers legal advice, solicited or not.

jeepers creepers! an interjection of surprise or delight.

The equivalent of "no kidding!" or "wow!" depending on the context, the phrase came from a 1938 popular song first sung by Louis "Sachmo" Armstrong in the movie *Going Places.* The chorus began, "Jeepers Creepers, where'd ya get those peepers? / Jeepers Creepers, where'd ya get those eyes?"

jerkwater town: a small community with modest conveniences.

Tracks along main lines in the early days of American railroading had permanent towers that supplied water for steam locomotives. Not so along less important routes, so train crews and any other willing hands had to form bucket brigades to fill the boiler from streams and ponds. Filling the buckets was known as "jerking water," and any small collection of houses, stores, and community buildings where that was done were "jerkwater towns."

The epithet stuck, especially when people from larger towns and cities wanted a snide way of referring to small towns. (See "one-horse town.")

jerry built: constructed in a cheap, ramshackle, or otherwise insubstantial fashion.

Although the phrase is widely thought to have come from the British World War I slang term for "German," it well antedates the 20th century. Some possibilities are an old English word for tumble, Jericho (as in Joshua causing the walls to come tumbling down).

Joe Blow: an ordinary person.

That phrase meant just an average guy—any old Joe ("Joe Doakes" was a variation). It was the predecessor of "Joe Sixpack." In fact, "Joe" was such a common first name (or nickname) that it became a slang word for coffee, which was also found everywhere.

Joe College: a typical male college student.

The phrase came on the scene in the 1930s, usually applied approvingly, but occasionally as a label for a student whom the academic life sheltered from having to hold down a "real job" in the "real world."

jot or tittle: the slightest change.

In the King James version of Matthew 5:18 we read, "For verily I say unto you, Till heaven and earth pass, one jot or one tittle shall in no wise pass from the law, till all be fulfilled." A "jot" was an iota, a very small quantity (we still use the expression "not one iota of truth"); a tittle was a tiny accent mark. Accordingly, to have said "not one jot or tittle" was a very erudite way of refusing to make even the most minor alteration.

⟡

"Just the facts, Ma'am": Don't embellish your story.

Many expressions moved from a movie or television program to popular speech, but none more quickly than a misquotation (as it turns out) of a lines by Sergeant Joe Friday, played by Jack Webb on the 1950s TV series *Dragnet.*

With his deadpan expression and staccato speech, Friday enthralled the public; *Dragnet* was one of the highest-rated drama series of the decade. At least once in every show, viewers heard Friday tell a female witness, "Just the facts, Ma'am."

Except they didn't. He might have said, "Give us the facts, ma'am," but he never uttered the four-word phrase. No matter, because the phrase swept the country in a wide range of contexts. If you wanted to be thought of (if only by yourself) as clever, you interjected "Just the facts, Ma'am" delivered in a Friday voice in a question or request.

Oh well, Humphrey Bogart's character Rick in the movie *Casablanca* never said "Play it again, Sam" either.

❧

K

"Katie, bar the door!": "Watch out—there's trouble coming!"

King James I, who was set upon in 1437 by unhappy Scots, took refuge in a room whose door had no bar lock. One Catherine Douglas tried to keep the door closed with her arm, but the mob broke through and murdered the king. That the king might have shouted, "Catherine, bar the door," is not too very different from the once-popular phrase.

That the expression was brought to America by Anglo-Scottish settlers is equally likely, and for generations rural folk would acknowledge a difficult situation with a shake of the head and "Katy, bar the door."

❧

keeping up with the Joneses: making an effort to match your neighbors' social and financial status.

If you bought a Chevrolet, but the guy who lived across the street bought a Cadillac, you wouldn't, vehicularly speaking, be considered in the same league. But if he took his wife and kids to Europe for a month and you took your wife and kids to Europe for a month, you were keeping up with the Joneses, no matter what your neighbor's last name was.

The phrase came from a 1913 newspaper carton strip "Keep with the Joneses," the name being as ubiquitous a last name as "Joe" was in phrases that used that first name. (See also "status seeker.")

❧

Keystone Kops: incompetence incarnate.

One of the staples of Mack Sennett's silent-movie comedies from World War I through the 1920s was a group of clumsily ineffective policemen known as the Keystone Kops (Keystone was the name of Sennett's film company). The Kops moved as a group, bumping into each other, driving their car in circles, and otherwise achieving nothing in the way of law enforcement but producing lots of movie mayhem.

As a phrase to describe a group that accomplished nothing after lots of effort, "Keystone Kops" would suit them to a T.

❧

kick over the traces: to disregard what is expected and follow your own wishes.

Traces are the leather harness straps by which a horse is attached to a wagon or another vehicle.

When the animal becomes upset, it may well kick out and end up stepping over the traces. At that point the driver has little or no control in steering or stopping.

A person who rebels against convention and acts in what society would consider an unseemly manner has kicked over the traces.

A similar equine-derived expression is "spit the bit and chuck the harness."

❧

kill the fatted calf: to hold a celebration, usually a long-awaited homecoming.

Luke 15:23 describes the return of the prodigal son as, "And bring here the fatted calf, and kill it; and let us eat, and be merry . . ."

Although the guest of honor in the biblical parable was a wastrel whose father welcomed home, "to kill the fatted calf" can refer to a party for anyone whom the host is pleased to see.

❧

Kilroy was here: a catch phrase that originated during World War II.

According to the most authoritative account of the phrase's origin, James Kilroy, who worked at a Massachusetts shipyard during the war, was in charge of counting rivets. He placed a chalk check mark on each block of rivets to ensure that they would not be counted more than once, but the workers, who were paid piecemeal, erased the mark once Kilroy left. After becoming aware of the problem, he added "Kilroy Was Here" and a drawing of a man peering over a fence. The new ships sailed before the rivet blocks could be painted, so the vessels spread the message that "Kilroy Was Here" throughout the war.

Soldiers and sailors adopted the phrase and it and the cartoon were scrawled on walls and other places wherever they went, contending that the graffiti was already there when they arrived.

Perhaps the unlikeliest place where the phrase was found was on an outhouse reserved for the use of Churchill, Stalin, and FDR during the 1945 Potsdam Conference. As the story goes, Stalin emerged after using the facility and asked an aide, "And who is Kilroy?"

❧

kit and caboodle: the entire thing.

A "kit" is a collection of items, such as a tool kit or a sewing kit. "Caboodle," comes from "boodle," is a collection of people. This 19th-century phrase was frequently misheard as "kitten caboodle," causing the mishearer to look around for a young feline.

knee high to a grasshopper: very young.

A grasshopper is tiny, and to stand, metaphorically speaking, no higher than the insect's knee was to be very small or young or both. The expression was usually used by male relatives to point out either a child's youth ("Drive the tractor by yourself?— why, you're not even knee-high to a grasshopper") or the speaker's experience ("I've driven tractors since I was knee high to a grasshopper").

knight in shining armor: a wonderful guy.

Fairy tales chronicled fair maidens in distress who were rescued at the last minute from dragons and ogres by a gallant knight in gleaming armor, whereupon they all lived happily ever after.

Even if a young woman didn't view herself as a princess or consider herself in desperate straits, she still imagined herself being carried off by the man of her dreams, Prince Charming, a knight in shining armor.

knuckle down: apply yourself to the job at hand.

The phrase comes from the game of marbles, one of the once-popular children's street games. Players shot their "shooter" marble by clenching the marble in a fist with knuckles touching the ground, then launching it with a flick of the thumb. When it was a player's turn and his attention was elsewhere, he was reminded, "Okay, knuckle down."

A similar phrase, "buckle down" most likely came from the idea of tightening your belt before performing an arduous task.

~

knuckle sandwich: a punch in the mouth.

Associated with urban street toughs, the phrase was common in "Dead End" and "Bowery Boys" movies where the threat of being served a meal of someone's fist was all part of the characters' bravado.

~

L

labor of Hercules: a very difficult task.

When the Greek hero Hercules was driven mad because of the goddess Hera's jealousy, he murdered his children. As atonement for his crime, he was obliged to perform twelve demanding tasks, such as slaying or capturing dangerous beasts, obtaining various prized and well-guarded possessions, and cleaning a very dirty stable in just one day. Hercules succeeded and was granted immortality and the hand of the now-mollified Hera's daughter.

If your boss gives you an impossible assignment, especially that must be completed in a short time, you could show off your classical education by referring to it as a labor of Hercules.

∽

"ladybug ladybug, fly away home": a chant to send a ladybug on its way.

The ladybug (or ladybird) beetle is helpful to farmers by reducing the number of harmful larvae and insects on crops. In certain parts of the English-speaking world, farmers chanted right before they burned their fields after harvest, "Ladybug ladybug, fly away home / Your house is on fire, your children alone [or your children are gone]."

Some people still recite the verse when a ladybug lands on them and before gently flicking the insect off them, because swatting a ladybug is considered very bad luck.

∽

the lady or the tiger: a problem with no solution.

Frank R. Stockton's short story titled "The Lady, or the tiger" is set in an ancient country whose king held an trial by ordeal. Behind one door was a beautiful woman; behind a second door was a ferocious tiger. Those on trial were forced to open one or the other door without knowing what was on the other side. To choose the one behind which was the woman meant the defendant was innocent, and he was obliged to marry the woman. However, to select the door behind which was the tiger was a sign of guilt, and the defendant would be eaten alive.

The king did not approve of his daughter's choice of suitor, who was forced to take the test. The princess knew what was behind both doors, and when her suitor looked to her for a hint, she was faced with a predicament: to indicate the maiden door would mean that her beloved would marry another; to point to the tiger door meant he would be killed.

What did the princess do? We'll never know, because Stockton ended the story just as the young man was about to open a door. All we were left with was a terrific phrase to describe any dilemma for which there is no satisfactory solution.

⌘

last hurrah: a final appearance, especially at the end of one's career.

The phrase has a bittersweet, if not sad, connotation, since it's applied to the end of a person's life's work. It could refer to a musical or theatrical performance or the end of a political career—the final time that the person will hear an audience or crowd shouting in praise.

"Swan song" (which see) has a similar meaning, although not always used in a positive sense.

&

lawn jockey: a derogatory term for an African-American.

A traditional feature of a Southern front yard was a statue of a diminutive black man painted in the colors of horseracing silks. His hand was outstretched, as if to hitch a horse's reins (the hand often ended in a ring for just that purpose).

As an expression connoting subservience in the sense of "slave" or "mascot," "lawn jockey" deserved to be consigned to the linguistic scrap heap.

&

lay on, Macduff: Go ahead and give it your best shot.

Macduff, a character in Shakespeare's *Macbeth*, correctly suspected Macbeth of murdering King Duncan. After Macbeth murders Macduff's family, Macduff leads an army against Macbeth. Their final confrontation includes Macbeth's challenging line: "Lay on, Macduff; / And damned be him that first cries, 'Hold, enough!'"

People who wanted to show off their erudition and wit simultaneously used the phrase in any "Go ahead!" context until it became through overuse a very tired cliché to which the best response is "Who's Leon Macduff?"

⚘

lead down garden path: deceive.
The path to which the phrase refers meant an intentional detour, so to escort someone down it was to mislead a person who relied on your honesty.

⚘

lick and a promise: a superficial effort.
Rather than wash themselves thoroughly to their parents' satisfaction, youngsters who were in a rush would splash on a little water and say they'd do a better job later. The phrase was extended to apply to any fast and incomplete job.

⚘

lie like a tombstone: to tell an untruth.
Epitaphs written on headstones often exaggerate the deceased's relationships, accomplishments, and even personal data. The dearly departed may not in fact have been "beloved by his family" or "a brave soldier" or even born in the year in which he did indeed first see the light of day. Therefore, "here lies" can have a dual meaning.

the life of Riley: a life of ease.

Although linguistic history fails to reveal who the eponymous Mr. Reilly was, the phrase was traced to the mid-19th century's Irish immigration to the United States. The phrase was used in popular songs and on the stage, and was most recently used as the title of a very successful radio program and later television series starring William Bendix as Chester A. Riley, whose signature comment, "What a revoltin' development this is," became a popular expression during the mid-20th century.

❧

Little Lord Fauntleroy: an effete and spoiled goody-two-shoes young man.

The youngster was the title character of the 19th-century novel by Frances Hodgson Burnett. He lived in New York City with his mother, the daughter of a British lord who had eloped to the States against the wishes of her father. Summoned to England, the lad wins over his grandfather's cold heart through his innate goodness and good sense and becomes heir to the title.

Although the title character was not at all spoiled or sissified, his hairstyle and clothing certainly gave that impression. That's why generations of privileged actual or supposed effete spoiled brats were taunted by sneers of "Look—here comes Little Lord Fauntleroy!"

⌒

live in a tree: to be lucky.

A '50s college expression, used in such contexts as telling a roommate whose exam for which he was unprepared was suddenly postponed: "Jeez, pal— you live in a tree."

⌒

lock horns: to get into an argument.

Two deer, moose, or members of another antlered species who have a dispute they want to settle will face off, paw the ground, and charge at each other. Their antlers clash and often become enmeshed. They have locked horns. People who have a bone to pick can be said to lock horns too.

The phrase appears in an 1865 poem by Algernon Swinburne to describe the domestic disagreement of a heifer and her mate locking horns.

⌒

lock, stock, and barrel: the whole thing.

A musket was made up of a flintlock mecha- nism that produced the power to launch the ball, a wooden stock that held the lock and the barrel, and the barrel through which the musket ball was propelled en route to its target. Put all three together and you have the whole shooting match.

The phrase was first used in the early 19th century to mean an entire entity or quantity.

⚬

long drink of water: a very tall person.

"Look at that basketball player—what a long drink of water!" The image is the distance that water would travel down the throat of someone of great height.

⚬

long-playing record: a 33 ⅓ rpm vinyl phonograph record.

Abbreviated LP, a long-playing record that was played at 33 revolutions per minute held more music than did a 45 rpm extended-play record or their 78 rpm shellac and later vinyl predecessor. A 16 rpm record never achieved much popularity.

⚬

Lord High Everything Else: someone who does a multitude of jobs.

Ko-Ko, a character in Gilbert and Sullivan's comic opera *The Mikado,* held the position of Lord High

Executioner. The only other town official was Pooh-Bah, who went by the title Lord High Everything Else.

Accordingly, if you're saddled with many jobs at your place of business, with or without accompanying titles, you may call yourself or be called "Lord High Everything Else." But no matter what you are called, your boss is still the grand Pooh-Bah.

⁊

long in the tooth: old.

Absent conclusive documentation, a horse's age is determined by the size and condition of its teeth, which show specific signs of growth or deterioration over the years. For example, a groove in an upper incisor usually first appears when a horse is ten, moves halfway down the tooth in five years, reaches the end in another five, and then begins to disappear.

There are far more flattering ways to refer to someone as being "long in the tooth"—to the extent that any reference to age is flattering—such as the French euphemism "a woman of a certain age."

⁊

loony bin: insane asylum.

The word "lunatic" comes from the word for "moon"; madness was associated in many cultures with the effect of the phases of the moon on the human mind. From lunatic came loony, and loony bin was where insane people were incarcerated.

The phrase is now considered insulting in the extreme, as are "booby hatch" (originally a covered passageway down a ship deck), "funny farm," "drool academy," and "foam rubber city" (a reference to padded cells).

⁓

lotus eater: someone whose only interests are luxury and sensual pleasures, a sybarite.

In *The Odyssey*, Odysseus and his crew encounter the Lotus Eaters, island inhabitants who spend their lives eating a narcotic that causes them to be drowsy and disinterested in anything but their own pleasure, sort of Homeric Flower Children.

Several crew members partook and had to be dragged back to the ship to which they were chained until they kicked the habit.

⁓

lounge lizard: a man interested in snaring a wealthy woman.

The phrase was first heard after World War I, when it was applied to musicians who performed in supper clubs and kept an eye out for susceptible women of means. As the century progressed, a man didn't have to be a musician; any well-dressed predatory male earned that phrase. Some say "lizard" referred to rep tile shoes that were popular footwear; other say the word applies to the men's low-life character.

"Lounge lizard" is the male equivalent of "gold digger."

❦

M

mad as a hatter: crazy.

The standard explanation comes from the effect to the brain caused by mercury nitrate used by 18th- and 19th-century hatmakers. Another view holds that "mad" originally meant "poisonous" and "hatter" is a corruption of the Saxon word "atter," the adder snake, the bite of which affects the brain.

In any event, the Mad Hatter character in Lewis Carroll's *Alice in Wonderland* is a testimony to eccentricity bordering on madness.

❦

mad as a March hare: crazy.

According to folklore, hares behave as though they're "sparring" with other hares and leaping around for no discernible reason during their breeding season. Their breeding season in Europe begins during the month of March.

main drag: the biggest or most important thoroughfare of a town or city.

"Drag" came from a term for a wagon or carriage that a horse would pull or drag. By extension the road on which the vehicle was dragged became a slang word for "street"—think of drag racing.

make whoopee: celebrate noisily; a genteelly humorous term for having intercourse.

In either chase, "whoopee" is the sound of enjoyment. "Makin' Whoopee" is the title of a 1928 hit song by Eddie Cantor, a cautionary tale in which the man in question goes from courtship to marriage to fatherhood and other responsibilities and finally to divorce.

man alive!: an expression of surprise or pleasure.

The phrase most likely arose as an alternative to something stronger, such as "Good lord!" which would have been acceptable to those people who objected to taking the deity's name in vain.

manner born: familiar with such things.

The phrase comes from *Hamlet*: "But to my mind, though I am native here. And to the manner born, it is a custom / More honour'd in the breach than the observance."

The widespread confusion between "manner and "manor" has been going on for at least two centuries. "To the manor born," in the sense of accustomed to luxury as if raised in an aristocratic environment, was used as the title of a British sitcom that achieved some popularity on American public television.

❧

matinee idol: a handsome male movie actor whose screen presence excites female audiences.

Although we now associate "matinee" with the legitimate theater, the word also applied to afternoon movie shows. Perhaps because housewives and young women constituted the largest audience segment at such screenings, any actor whose appearance evoked sighs and other expressions of female approval became known as a matinee idol, regardless of his acting ability.

That is not to say that a matinee idol was necessarily a bad actor, but his looks were the defining characteristic.

❧

Maybees don't fly in June: Stop changing your mind so much.

"Maybees" is a pun on "maybes," as in "If I do X, then maybe Y will happen, but if I don't do X, then maybe Z will happen . . I just can't decide." When someone used to hesitate in such a fashion, someone else would be sure to pipe up with the reminder that "maybes don't fly in June."

❧

mean enough to steal a penny off a dead man's eyes: very mean.

To keep a deceased's eyes closed, undertakers or whoever tended the body placed coins on the eyes. Anyone who would steal the money was indeed reprehensible.

Just as evil was a man who was "mean enough to steal his wife's egg money," pin money earned from selling eggs that the family didn't use themselves.

❧

method to one's madness: do things in an unorthodox fashion, yet nevertheless achieve the intended result.

Yet again Shakespeare's *Hamlet* provided a phrase that was picked up and used through the ages. Having observed Hamlet rave on in what appeared to be senseless sentences, Polonious makes a comment that turns out to be true: "Though this be madness, yet there is method in't." Under less dramatic circumstances, the phrase applies to getting the right outcome by what seems to be the wrong method, and we've all done that.

milk of human kindness: compassion or benevolence.

Shakespeare again, but this time *Macbeth*. Lady Macbeth regrets that her husband doesn't have the overwhelming ambition that she has by saying, "Yet do I fear thy nature, It is too full o' th' milk of human kindness. To catch the nearest way."

Macbeth heeds his wife, schemes and murders his way to the throne, and is then deposed and killed. The milk must have curdled.

A compliment to a sweetheart of a person is to say that he or she is "full of the milk of human kindness."

❧

mind your own beeswax: a euphemism for "mind your own business."

Since "mind their own business" sounds harsh, if not impolite, the close-sounding word "beeswax" was substituted. Those to whom the remark was directed might still get their noses out of joint, but somewhat less so than if the word had been "business."

An interesting, although fanciful, piece of folk etymology tells us that American colonial women stood over a kettle and stirred wax to make candles. If they didn't pay attention, the wax or fire might burn their hair and clothing. Someone who let her concentration wander would be reminded to "mind your own beeswax."

⁓

mind your p's and q's: behave yourself.

Opinion is divided over what the letters in the admonition to "mind your p's and q's" mean. They might have been two similar-looking letters that typesetters were warned not to confuse. They might have stood for pints and quarts that tavern keepers could have confused.

Neither, however, is close to the idea of being on your best behavior, but *p* standing for "please" and *q* for "thank you" (pronounced thank-kew) does. And that's how generations of parents reminded their children to remember their manners.

⁓

moment of truth: a crucial test.

Unless a matador is injured or loses his nerve before the end of a bullfight, the climax comes when he reaches over the horns to plunge his sword behind the animal's neck. The matador is then at his most vulnerable, since the bull need only raise its head to gore the man.

This "moment of truth" when a matador reveals whether he has sufficient courage is a literal translation of the Spanish phrase for that point in time. By extension, any situation in which a person is called on to show "the right stuff" can be called the moment of truth.

❧

monkey's uncle: an impossibility.

Charles Darwin's theory of evolution, especially the notion that man was descended from apes, was greeted with much skepticism, and especially in parts of the English-speaking world where Creationism held sway.

Hence the expression "Well, I'll be a monkey's uncle," which was used to show grave doubts about any and all seemingly improbable situations.

Another animal phrase used by doubters and scorners was "when pigs fly."

❧

in the arms of Morpheus: asleep.

Morpheus, son of Hypnos, the Greek god of sleep, was the god of dreams. He lent his name to morphine and to the pretentiously classical allusion "in the arms of Morpheus."

❧

Mrs. Astor's plush horse: ostentatious.

Mrs. William Astor, the leader of New York society at the end of the 19th century, was not one to spare any expense in clothing, furnishings, or other accoutrements of the Good Life (so much for the idea of quiet old money). Her appearance and her gala parties were so sumptuous and well-known that anyone who appeared dolled up beyond normal was ridiculed as "Astor's plush [or pet] horse," as if the formidable Mrs. A had lavished her wealth on that person as she would on a favorite plaything.

❧

mutual admiration society: two or more people who lavishly praise the other person's or people's personalities and accomplishments, often far beyond what is deserved.

The phrase, which is said to have originated with Henry David Thoreau in 1851, may have been used earlier. Its use as the title of a song from the 1956 musical comedy *Happy Hunting* that was successfully recorded by a number of singers boosted the phrase's popularity.

❧

N

nail polish on a hangnail: ugly or useless despite an attractive appearance.

This phrase, which is most often heard in "You can put nail polish on a hangnail, but it's still a hangnail," can be used in all sorts of situations . . . and for all sorts of people.

❦

naked as a jaybird: stark naked.

Why, of all ornithological species, should a jaybird be singled out for its nudity? One explanation is that "jay" was a 19th-century word for a country bumpkin, and since bumpkins were vulnerable to the wiles of others, a jaybird would be vulnerable indeed.

❦

(your/his/her) name is mud: a dishonored reputation.

Folk etymology would have it that "mud" is really "Mudd," as in Dr. Samuel Mudd, the physician who was imprisoned for conspiring with John Wilkes Booth and then treating Booth's broken leg following Lincoln's assassination.

However, the phrase was recorded some twenty years before Lincoln died. In truth, one 19th-century meaning of "mud" was a fool (as in a rustic clodhopper), not a good epithet to have attached to your good name.

❦

necking knob: a swivel on a car's steering wheel

The necking knob enables the driver to steer with his left hand while encircling his girlfriend's shoulder with his right arm. Even when the driver was alone, the knob was an easy way to turn the car in the days before power steering.

☙

neither rhyme nor reason: making no sense at all.

"Rhyme" alludes to poetry and by extension all of the creative arts, while "reason" stands for intellect. Accordingly, something that can't be understood or justified in terms of either artistic merit or logic is indeed of little value.

☙

ne plus ultra: the highest point of excellence, acme.

Loosely translated from the Latin for "there is no reason to go further," the phrase is a synonym of "zenith." A new car with all the most modern features that any buyer could wish for (or so the manufacturer claims) might be touted as the ne plus ultra of automobiles.

Legend has it that "ne plus ultra"—in its literal sense—was inscribed on Gibraltar's Pillars of Hercules as a warning to mariners not to venture, depending on the direction in which they were sailing, into the Atlantic Ocean or the Mediterranean Sea.

♨

"Nice play, Shakespeare!": a sarcastic observation on someone's dumb behavior.

Similarly, "Smooth move, ExLax!"

♨

nine day wonder: something with short-lived popularity.

The idea is that a song, a fad, or anything else that captures the public's fancy starts out like a house on fire but begins to pall after a little more than a week. The proverb "A wonder lasts nine days, and then the puppy's eyes are open" refers to dogs being born with their eyes shut; like them, the public is blind to the fad until they become sated or bored or both and then their eyes metaphorically open.

The earliest recorded use of the phrase came from William Kemp, an Elizabethan comic actor, who in 1600 did a Morris dance over the 130 miles from London to Norwich. His account of his nine-day dance-athon was titled *Kemp's Nine Daies Wonder,* which would suggest that the phrase had been well in vogue before Kemp used it.

no dice: an absolute refusal.

According to one explanation, courts would not convict gamblers at illegal craps games unless they were caught with dice (swallowing the evidence was not an uncommon way to get rid of it). "No dice, no conviction" was the watchword that referred to that refusal to convict.

no rest for the wicked: perpetual torment.

We are told in Isaiah 57:21 that "there is no peace, saith my God to the wicked." The phrase is often said as "no rest for the weary" and heard as a mild complaint in labor-intensive situations.

Now you're on the trolley!: Now you catch on.

"Trolley" refers to the streetcars that predated buses and subways in major cities. To flounder around to the answer to a question or how to perform some sort of procedure and then to come up with the right answer was the equivalent of getting on a trolley that's on the right track (as in track of streetcar rails).

O

odd's bodkins: an archaic interjection meaning "God's body."

In an era where people respected the Ten Commandments a lot more than we do today, the injunction against taking the name of the Lord in vain led to a variety of euphemisms. One involved using the word "bodkins," the tools that shoemakers and other leatherworkers use to pierce holes, for "body." The most convincing explanation is that "bodkins" sounds a lot like "body," but there's no explanation for the plural. Therefore, when a cobbler hit his thumb while resoling a shoe, he was likely to wince and exclaim, "Odd's bodkins," if not something worse.

Henry Fielding was the first author to use the phrase in close to its present form in his *Don Quixote in England*: "Odsbodlikins . . . you have a strange sort of a taste."

Similar oaths that avoided naming the diety used "'s" as an abbreviation of "God's," such as "s'wounds," "s'blood," and "s'truth." However, it's unlikely that Ira Gershwin had that in mind when he wrote the lyrics to "S'Wonderful."

the old gray mare: the passage of time.

A folk song attributed to Stephen Foster and supposedly referring to a 19th-century harness-racing horse named Lady Suffolk begins, "Oh, the old gray mare, she ain't what she used to be . . . Many long years ago."

Unkind people used the image to refer women "of a certain age" (or older), although when used by themselves about themselves, it has an air of self-deprecating resignation. For example, a middle-aged woman who leaves the dance floor short of breath after a vigorous jitterbug may wipe her brow, reach for a cold drink, and exclaim, "The old gray mare ain't what she used to be."

◦᨞

old school tie: a social or business network of graduates of a secondary school, college, or university in which the members help each other because of their common bond.

Among the sartorial details of the Harry Potter movies were the distinctive striped neckties that represented each house. The ties echoed those worn by students at real-life British boarding schools and universities and at American prep schools and colleges. Many alumni continue to sport the neckwear for the rest of their lives to show their academic heritage and to allow themselves to be recognized by fellow graduates.

Small wonder, then, that this feeling of pride and sense of community makes these alumni kindly disposed to their colleagues, willing if not eager to help them find employment or membership and to gain advancement. In that sense, "tie" refers both to the cravat and to the interpersonal relationship.

A similar expression, "old boy network," comes from the British expression for a graduate of certain upper-crust boarding schools: As a graduate of Eton, James Bond was an Eton old boy.

ॐ

one fell swoop: a single and rapid act.

"Fell" comes from an Old English word for frightful and "swoop" describes the way hawks and other birds of prey drop out of the sky to capture their victims. Accordingly, something that is done "in one fell swoop," whether or not it is awful, happens with no hesitation.

Shakespeare coined the phrase in *Macbeth*, where the character Macduff laments the murders of his wife and children with "What, all my pretty chickens and their dam / At one fell swoop?"

૱

one man's meat is another man's poison: you may not like something that I like.

The phrase, which was first written by the Roman poet Lucretius, was appropriated to refer to any situation where two people disagree over something.

The 20th-century literary wit George S. Kauffman's most celebrated pun was "One man's Mede is another man's Persian."

O tempora! O mores!: Oh, the times, oh, the customs!

This Latin phrase comes from an oration of Cicero, in which he bitterly denounced the corruption of the Rome of his day. It was subsequently used by the erudite to criticize their own era. Quote Cicero if you wish, but be prepared to be greeted by blank or at least quizzical stares . . . more than half your listeners will think you're complaining about a Japanese restaurant's tempura.

૱

out of whole cloth: fictitious.

The most convincing explanation for this phrase deals with Middle Ages tailors who wove fabric on large looms, then cut the pieces into suits and dresses.

Garments made from a single bolt of cloth were far preferable to ones made from leftover pieces.

Dishonest tailors tried to convince customers that their clothes were made of whole cloth. When their lie was found out enough times, "whole cloth" came to stand for a fabrication, the meaning that survives to this day.

❧

P

palooka: a stupid or a clumsy oaf, and by extension, an incompetent prizefighter.

Joe Palooka, the heavyweight boxing hero of Ham Fisher's cartoon strip that ran from 1921 to 1984, was anything but inept, but even his skills and the strip's popularity couldn't save the word from its negative meaning.

Calling someone a "big palooka," unless said in a jovial and friendly context, isn't likely to win you any fans and may win you a bloody nose.

The word may have been a corruption of "Pollack," the pejorative term for Polish people.

❧

Pandora's box: a receptacle of woes and evils.

According to Greek legend, Pandora, the first woman on Earth, was given a jar (it became "box" in the phrase) that she was instructed never to open. Curiosity overcame her, however, and when she lifted the lid, all the evils of the world flew out, not unlike to Eve's eating the forbidden fruit.

Someone who does something that leads to widespread disaster is said to have opened a Pandora's box.

৵

paper tiger: something that appears dangerous but is not.

The phrase comes from a Chinese expression that means what it does in English—something or someone that is all bark but no bite. The phrase is often used in international diplomacy to describe a nation that makes threats but is unlikely to back them up with action.

৵

pardon my French: please excuse my language.

In the days when language propriety was more of an issue than it is now, using a word or phrase that was "unfit for mixed company" was likely to lead to embarrassment. Since French was considered a racy language, people excused themselves with "pardon my French."

parting shot: the last word.

At the end of a heated discussion or argument, you unleash a zinger of a remark as you leave. You've just made a parting shot.

The phrase is very often said as "Parthian shot." The Parthians were a Persian tribe that developed the cavalry tactic of retreating in order to draw their enemy after them, whereupon they would turn in the saddle and fire a barrage of arrows. Although some scholars say "parting" came from "Parthian," others say it's coincidental.

party line: communal telephone service.

In the early days of telephone service, two or more households shared a circuit to the same central switchboard at the phone company. The operator would alert the recipient of an incoming call by a distinctive ring (say, two longs and a short), which distinguished that party from others in the line.

"Shared service" meant just that. Since only one call at a time could be made or received, hogging the line led to bad feelings and sometimes bad language from other households who wanted to use the phone. Another problem was eavesdropping, the premise of the classic movie comedy *Pillow Talk*.

pay the piper: be forced to acknowledge and accept an unpleasant consequence of your action.

The full expression is "Who pays the piper calls the tune," which is to say that money calls the shots ("Money makes the mare go" is the same idea). But although a request can be melodious, the phrase came to have an unpleasant connotation, as if the music that the piper produced was not what was anticipated.

For example, you tell your supervisor and your colleagues that you can undertake and finish an important assignment in two days, but you can't. As your supervisor takes you to task, you silently admit that you bit off more than you could chew—you're paying the piper.

peanut gallery: a rowdy audience.

The original peanut galleries were the cheapest, which is to say, the highest, seats in a theater or vaudeville house. Their patrons heckled and often threw peanuts (the least expensive items sold at the snack bar) at performers who didn't measure up to the audience's expectations.

The most popular children's television show of the mid-20th century was *Howdy Doody* (Howdy, Mr. Bluster, Flub-A-Dub and other marionettes interacted with their human friends led by Buffalo Bob Smith and Clarabelle the Clown). The studio audience were children who sat in the Peanut Gallery and were encouraged to laugh, cheer, or boo at the show's riotous happenings.

❧

pearls before swine: wasting something that is not appreciated.

In Matthew 7:6, Jesus warned his followers not to waste time by throwing pearls of wisdom before ungodly swine.

When writers Claire Booth Luce and Dorothy Parker simultaneously arrived at a door, Luce stepped back to allow Parker to precede her by saying with a smile, "Age before beauty." As she walked through the door, Parker replied, "And pearls before swine."

❧

Peck's bad boy: a mischief maker.

"Peck's Bad Boy" was the nickname of Hennery, a character created by 19th-century newspaperman George Wilbur Peck. Hennery played pranks on friends, neighbors, and especially his alcoholic father. These stories were later compiled into books, and the character of Hennery appeared in a number of early motion pictures.

The phrase "Peck's bad boy" was applied to someone, usually a youngster, whose impish behavior plagued those around him.

෴

peep show: a short soft-core porn exhibition.

To enjoy "forbidden" glimpses of naked female flesh, a man went to an arcade in a sleazy neighborhood, paid his dime or quarter, entered a booth, and stared through a peep hole at a partially or fully unclothed woman. The "show," which lasted for no more than five or ten minutes, began when a shade or other obstruction over the peep hole was raised and ended when it was lowered.

Instead of "live models," some peep shows featured short films shown on individual viewing machines.

Peep shows became less and less commercially viable as movie houses (and now the Internet) showed more explicit fare.

෴

person to person: a phone call for which the intended party was changed only when the intended caller answered the phone.

Back in the days before inexpensive or free long-distance phone calls, callers worried about the risk of being charged if the person to whom they wanted to speak wasn't available. To avoid that possibility, they made an operator-assisted person-to-person call. However, if they wanted to gamble or they knew the party would be available to answer, they made a station-to-station call where toll charges began when anyone picked up the receiver.

Many travelers abused person-to-person calls to let the folks at home know that they had reached their destination. For example, college students placed calls to a family pet when they returned to a distant school after vacation. Their parents knew their children had arrived safely when they received a person-to-person call for "Mr. Spot" or "Ms. Fluffy."

༶

Philadelphia lawyer: an adept attorney.

The most probable reason why the City of Brotherly Love became an adjective for astute and skillful lawyers was Andrew Hamilton, whose 1735 defense of printer John Peter Zenger was a milestone of freedom of the press in America. (Lawyer Andrew should not be confused with Secretary of the Treasury Alexander Hamilton.)

༶

Although the Zenger trial was held in New York City, Hamilton was from Philadelphia. Curiously, it took some fifty years for the phrase to appear in print.

❧

pig in a poke: an item bought without prior inspection.

A poke is a "bag." Purchasing something that you've not seen is the basis of the image—you don't know the condition of the pig in the bag until after you've bought it. It may be exactly what was advertised, or it may be something much worse than what the seller described—the swine!

❧

in a pig's eye: untrue.

"Eye" is a rhyme for "lie." "Pig" has an unpleasant connotation. Put them together, and you have an expression for something that's patently false.

The phrase was most often heard as a rejoinder to a remark that the hearer believes is untrue. To the statement that "The Cubs will win the World Series next year" might well be the response, "In a pig's ear."

Or, to use another porcine phrase, "When pigs fly."

police blotter: a precinct's daily written record of arrests.

In the days before ballpoint pens, much less computers, police station house records were kept with ink pens, the writing from which had to be blotted to keep the ink from smearing. Sheets of paper might come and go, but the blotter's indelible imprint remained as a metaphorical reminder of the name of the person who was arrested. That's why many old gangster movies has lines about the cops checking a bad guy's record on the police blotter.

pony up: pay the money.

"Pony" has nothing to do with small equines—it comes from *pone*, the Latin word for "put" (so does the Spanish verb *poner*). Therefore, if you owe someone money, you'd better pony up.

poor as Job's turkey: poverty-stricken.

The biblical Job's hardships did not bode well for any barnyard creatures that depended on him for sustenance. This wonderfully descriptive old Southern phrase says all that needs to be said about some one in dire financial straits.

ॐ

poor little rich girl: unhappy heiress.

In contrast to Job's turkey, the subject of this phrase wants for nothing—except emotional support.

The original "poor little rich girl" was socialite Barbara Hutton, heiress to the Woolworth ("Five and Dime" stores) and E. F. Hutton investment banking fortunes. She had a lonely childhood, seven failed—and in many cases, exploitive—marriages, and died a broken (and nearly broke) woman at age sixty-six.

The phrase has been applied to other women whose lives were sad in spite (or perhaps because of inherited wealth).

possession is nine-tenths of the law: custody presumes ownership.

The basis of this legal maxim that comes down from the 17th-century is the commonsense observation that if you have control of something, chances are better than average that it's yours. Lawyers term it a rebuttable presumption: ownership is recognized unless disproved by someone holding a more valid claim.

The phrase started life as "possession is nine points of the law," which referred to possession's satisfying nine out of eleven factors that constituted absolute ownership. However, "nine-tenths" entered popular usage to reflect the idea that custody is 90 percent of legal ownership.

❧

pretty kettle of fish: irritating or embarrassing situation.

The Scottish tradition of community fish-boil dinners often degenerated in brawls, to the extent that people began to refer to the events by this sarcastic phrase. Fish-boils may have evaporated, but the expression and the sarcasm haven't.

❧

Procrustean solution: adjusting the facts to suit the situation.

In Greek mythology, Procrustes (his name meant "stretcher") lived in a roadside house in which he invited travelers for a meal and a night's rest. The guests stayed in a bed whose length, according to Procrustes, exactly matched anyone who slept in it. And it did—after the host stretched a smaller guest on a rack or chopped the legs off a taller guest until he fit the bed. This practice ended only when the hero Theseus killed Procrustes by giving him a dose of his own medicine.

Someone who alters the facts by, for example, overestimating or underreporting data is said to offer a Procrustean solution.

⚬

pull a cork: have a drink.

This expression dates from the days when home-brewed potent potables were stored in large jugs with cork stoppers. A suggestion that the contents be shared might have been phrased as "Hey, neighbor, you about ready to pull that cork?"

⚬

pull up stakes: to move, usually one's home.

This phrase was first used by Virginia colonists in the early 17th century. Jamestown and other settlements were surrounded by wooden palisade stakes as a defense against marauding Native Americans. To change or expand one's residence would have meant moving the barriers too, much easier than to rebuild from scratch.

The phrase is sometimes heard as "pick up stakes." The opposite is "put down stakes."

The British equivalent is "up sticks," the sticks referring to army tent pegs.

❧

puppy love: a juvenile crush, an infatuation.

The phrase refers to an adolescent male's total devotion to the object of his affection by displaying the uncritical ardor of a young dog to its owner. "Mooning over" and "calf eyes" are apt phrases for such an affliction.

The 1960s teen singing idol Neil Sedaka had a hit record of a song by that name.

❧

put through the ringer: subjected to a harsh scolding or punishment.

Before washing machine spin cycles, excess water was squeezed out of hand-washed laundry by means of a wringer mounted on an agitator-type washing machine or a sink. The device was composed of two cylinders set close together and turned by a hand crank.

Being put through the wringer could be hard on delicate clothing, and being put through the metaphorical wringer, such as being chewed out by your boss, isn't much fun either.

❦

putting on the Ritz: acting in a pretentiously stylish and affluent manner.

César Ritz, founder of the Hotel Ritz in Paris and Ritz Hotel in London, lent his name to these and other highly fashionable institutions. To behave as if you belonged in such opulent settings and demand that you be treated as if you did would lead to being accused of "putting on the Ritz" or simply being "ritzy."

The phrase is best known as the title of a 1929 Irving Berlin song that has been performed by, among other, Fred Astaire, Judy Garland, and Peter Boyle (as the monster in Mel Brooks' movie *Young Frankenstein*).

A similar expression is "putting on the dog," coming perhaps from high collars and jeweled chokers known as "dogs."

❦

Q

on the Q.T.: confidentially.

"Q.T." is simply a shortened form of the word "quiet." You're being told something on the Q.T. is to be asked to keep it under your hat.

⁓

Queer Street: shaky on one's feet.

This British phrase originally meant to have fallen on hard financial times. It was appropriated by the American prizefighting community to describe a boxer who, having been knocked down, stands up slowly, and wobbles on rubbery legs while wondering, "Who am I and where am I?"—such a pug is on Queer Street.

⁓

Quiz Kid: a very smart youngster.

A popular radio show during the 1940s and '50s and later a television series, *Quiz Kids* featured a panel of five youngsters, none over the age of sixteen, with extraordinarily high IQs. They answered difficult questions on a wide range of topics that were submitted by listeners. Among the panelists who went on to bigger and better things was James Watson, the Nobel scientist who codiscovered DNA.

People used the phrase as both a compliment ("My son is so smart, he could be a Quiz Kid") and sarcasm ("You flunked another test?—nice going, Quiz Kid!").

⁓

R

rack and ruin: completely destroyed.

"Rack" is a variant of "wrack," meaning "wreck." Accordingly, something (or someone) that has gone to rack and ruin is totally devastated.

⁂

read between the lines: infer an unexpressed meaning.

An early method of transmitting written coded messages was to write the secret information in invisible ink between the lines of a document. The recipient would then learn the information by reading between the lines.

The phrase came to mean gaining an insight in the context of reading something into another person's words or behavior—and often both. For example, you, your spouse, and teenage son are invited to a family gathering. Your son's reaction when he heard the news was to stare at the floor and mutter, "Well, okay if I gotta." Reading between the lines, you'd say that he's not crazy about going.

⁂

read 'em and weep!: You won't be happy with this news.

You're playing poker, and at the end of a hand you hold a full house, aces high. Only you and another player are left in the round. You lay down your hand, and just as you're about to reach for the substantial amount of money in the pot, the other player lays down his cards and says smugly, "Read 'em and weep." It's a straight flush.

Although the phrase is most commonly heard in card games, it has been used in other situations, such as when a garage mechanic with a distorted sense of humor hands you a staggeringly large bill for his services.

કરી

read the riot act: criticize harshly.

A 1725 British Act of Parliament provided that a magistrate could tell any gathering of a dozen or more people who were creating a civil disturbance to disperse by reading an official statement to that effect. Failure to heed the warning led to arrest (the law remained in effect until 1973).

Used popularly, the phrase became the equivalent of "getting a good chewing out," even if only one person was "read the riot act."

કરી

red herring: a misleading clue.

Many people who know the phrase believe it came from the practice of game poachers laying scents of smoked herring (smoking accounted for the fish's reddish color) to throw gamekeepers and their dogs off the poachers' scent. However, etymologists discount that explanation, favoring instead that the phrase originated with an English writer who used the scent-laying image as a metaphor for a particular political plan.

Mystery writers, readers, and critics use "red herring" to describe a piece of plotting intended to throw the reader off in deducing who-done-it. The financial world uses the phrase to mean a stock prospectus, not from any intent to deceive, but because the document has a red cover.

◈

the real McCoy: the genuine article.

No one is certain how "McCoy" came to stand for authenticity. It may refer to a Scottish clan leader named McKay; a prizefighter named Kid McCoy, who had a rival with the same name; or a bootlegger whose wares were what he claimed they were.

◈

reap the whirlwind: suffer the consequences.

Hosea 8:7's "For they have sown the wind, and they shall reap the whirlwind" has come to mean that evil deeds in the past will come back to haunt you. Another biblical verse with a similar admonition is Galatians 6:7's "Whatsoever a man soweth, that shall he also reap" (used as the expression, "you'll reap what you sow"), and Proverbs 11:29's "He that troubleth his own house shall inherit the wind."

As yet another indication how popular references have shifted from the sacred to the profane, the contemporary equivalent is "Be aware of what you do, or else it may come back and bite you in the ass."

ॐ

red-hot mama: a woman who is sexy in a flashy and obvious way.

The phrase reached its maximum popularity through an early 20th-century entertainer named Sophie Tucker, who billed herself as "the Last of the Red Hot Mamas" (history fails to reveal who was the first). Nothing about her was shy or demure—one of her songs began, "You've got to see Mama ev'ry night or you can't see Mama at all."

As a description of a woman who appealed to male carnal appetites, the phrase was used by men and often, like Ms. Tucker, by the women themselves.

ॐ

rest on one's laurels: to stop participating because of satisfaction with past achievements.

The ancient Greeks crowned their victorious athletes and poets with wreaths made from the laurel bush, as did the Romans to honor their triumphant generals.

People who have in their own estimation been sufficiently successful and retire from whatever endeavor they were successful in are said to be resting on their laurels.

❧

richer than Croesus: very wealthy.

Croesus ruled an ancient Asia Minor kingdom who amassed a fabulous amount of wealth (he is also credited with having minted the first gold coins). How he would have compared to computer moguls and hedge-fund tycoons can never be measured, but his name lived on as someone who wasn't worried about where his next meal was coming from.

"Rockefeller" was the late 19th- and 20th-century comparison: "He spends money like he's Rockefeller." A Chock Full O' Nuts commercial included the line "better coffee Rockefeller's millions can't buy" until the Rockefeller family requested a change to "better coffee a millionaire's money can't buy."

⚬

rich beyond the dream of avarice: wealthy beyond imagination.

"Avarice" means "greedy," so to be rich beyond the dream of avarice is to have more money than even a Scrooge McDuck or Charles Montgomery Burns nocturnal fantasy.

The phrase can be traced back to two 18th-century writers, the redoubtable Samuel Johnson and the lesser-known Edward Moore.

⚬

ride a tiger: to find yourself in a precarious situation.

The phrase comes from "He who rides a tiger is afraid to dismount." Which is to say, once you find yourself in a dangerous circumstance, getting out of it can be even more potentially hazardous, whether to your health or your career.

⚬

rob Peter to pay Paul: use funds from one source to repay a debt.

If you use one credit card to pay off another, even if you're benefiting by buying time, you're robbing Peter to pay Paul. How the phrase came to be associated with what would seem to be the two apostles is a mystery, since neither was associated with precarious financial planning.

⚬꙰⚬

rogues gallery: collection of "head shot" photographs.

A rogues gallery is a compilation of "mug shot" photos of actual and suspected criminals maintained by police departments for purposes of identification. The practice began in the mid-19th century with the development of photography.

By extension, any collection of head-and-shoulder photos, such as college fraternity composites and academic yearbooks, is jokingly referred to as rogues galleries.

⚬꙰⚬

round heels: promiscuous.

The image is that of a woman who is such a push-over that the heels of her shoes became rounded from her being pushed over backwards so frequently. The phrase was popular in men's dormitories and barracks until the sexual revolution changed attitudes.

Other obsolescent phrases and expressions were "a scarlet woman," "a woman of easy virtue," "loose [or "low"] morals," a "tramp." On the other hand, men were applauded for being a "lady's man," a "cocksman," a "Romeo," or a "Casanova," all of which demonstrate which gender controlled the language.

S

Sadie Hawkins Day: ladies choice.

A character in Al Capp's Lil' Abner comic strip, Sadie Hawkins was reputedly the homeliest girl in the hillbilly town of Dogpatch. Eager to see her married off, her father instituted a footrace in which all of the town's unmarried girls pursued eligible bachelors— Daisy Mae's enticing Lil' Abner to the altar was an ongoing theme of the strip's plot.

As is often the case, nature imitates art, and by the late 1930s real live Sadie Hawkins Day events took place at many colleges and high schools, with girls taking the initiative and inviting boys to dances, dinner, and other events. Even at proms, hops, and other social events, one or more "Sadie Hawkins" dances allowed women to ask any man to take a turn on the dance floor.

༺༻

sacred cow: above criticism.

Hindus regard bovines as revered creatures, not to be mistreated in any way. The English-speaking world began to apply this religious practice in the mid-19th century to any person or project (often political in nature) that, like Caesar's wife (which see), should not be faulted.

༺༻

salad days: a time of youthful inexperience and carefree pleasures, usually looked back on with nostalgia.

The phrase came from Shakespeare's *Anthony and Cleopatra*, in which the Queen of the Nile reflected on "My salad days / When I was green in judgment: cold in blood . . ."

ఎం

salt mines: humorous characterization of one's job.

Salt deposits are often found underground, and even in the last century prisoners were condemned to long years or lifetimes of excavating the substance.

Little wonder that it became a metaphor for hard or otherwise unpleasant work, as in, as you return to the office after lunch, "Well, it's back to the salt mines."

ఎం

save for a rainy day: provide contingency funds for when times are tough.

There's no clear answer to when this expression began (some have traced it back to the 16th century), but it's clear that a "rainy day" is the symbol of gloom. The wise course, therefore, is to sock away funds to tide you over when times are tough.

ఎం

Say it ain't so, Joe: Your admitting your mistake would break my heart.

"Shoeless" Joe Jackson was involved in the "Black Sox" baseball scandal in which eight Chicago White Sox players were accused of fixing the 1919 World Series.

Legend has it that as Jackson was leaving the courthouse, a young fan tugged on his sleeve and, in a voice full of emotion, said, "Say it ain't so, Joe."

When Jackson confirmed the accusation, the lad realized that his idol had feet of clay.

❧

scarce as hen's teeth: nonexistent.

Hens have no teeth, so what could possibly be scarcer? (Stones in their gizzards act as teeth to grind their food).

❧

scattered from here to breakfast: in disarray.

It's been suggested that something that is total disorder would take the rest of the day and all through the night—that is, until breakfast—to correct.

Also heard as "from Hell to breakfast."

❧

second fiddle: play a less important role.

In an orchestra or string quartet, music produced by the second violin(s) tends to play more of a supportive harmonic role than the more melodically prominent first violin player(s) play.

By extension, "second fiddle" is a companion whose role is less recognized than the person who gets the credit.

⁊

See you later, alligator: Bye!

The title of a 1950s rock-'n'-roll smash hit by Bill Haley and His Comets, the phrase was already in use, especially in the South.

For a decade or more, hep/hip/with-it cats and chicks ended conversations with the phrase. The standard reply was the song's next line: "after a while, crocodile."

⁊

set her cap: a woman's determination to attract a particular man.

In the days when women's attire included head coverings, a woman who wanted to appeal to a man would wear her best bonnet. The phase was well-known in the 18th century, when Jane Austen used it in *Sense and Sensibility*: "1 abhor every commonplace phrase by which wit is intended; and 'setting one's cap at a man,' or 'making a conquest,' are the most odious of all."

⁓

seventh heaven: pure happiness.

Both Judaism and Islam recognize seven levels of heaven, of which the highest one is where God resides. To be in seventh heaven is therefore to experience ultimate bliss, whether theological or not.

⁓

shank's mare: walking.

"Shank" is another word for shinbone. By extension, its use in the phase refers to our legs. "Mare" here is equine transport, and when we walk, we "ride" on shank's mare.

⁓

shell shock: psychological adverse reaction to combat.

The phrase originated during World War I when intensive enemy artillery bombarding caused soldiers in the trenches to suffer from a variety of traumas that ranged from moderate panic attacks to physical and emotional paralysis.

Changes in warfare and psychological lingo caused the phrase to be replaced during the Second World War by "battle fatigue" and more recently to "post-traumatic stress disorder."

❧

short arms inspection (or drill): military inspection for venereal diseases.

Beginning with World War II, the military made visual determinations with regard to sexually transmitted diseases (primarily gonorrhea) through what was called a short arms inspection (or drill). Held early in the morning, men dressed in only their boots, helmet liners, and overcoat were summoned out of their barracks or bunks and ordered to line up. When indicated by the medical officer, each man opened his coat to bare his penis, which he then "milked" in a stripping motion to show whether there was any infectious discharge.

The term distinguished between a man's government-issued firearm and his own "short arm." The inspection practice ended after the Vietnam conflict.

❧

shotgun wedding: a wedding made compulsory by bride's pregnancy.

At a time and in social circles where a baby's illegitimacy stigmatized both mother and child, something had to be done, and in a hurry. As soon as his unwed daughter broke the news of her pregnancy and the father-to-be's unwillingness to marry her, the father grabbed his shotgun off the wall. With such motivation, the young man was forced to accompany the young lady to the nearest preacher or justice of the peace to make her an honest woman.

The phase is sometimes used to describe business mergers made only for reasons of expediency.

∾

shrinking violet: a shy person.

The violet flower gives the impression of shyness, growing as it does close to the protective ground and often beneath other plants, shrubs and trees. Compared to other larger foliage, violets do seem to look as though they are shrinking, growing smaller.

As applied to shy people, the phrase first appeared in both America and Great Britain in the 1820s.

∾

shuffle off this mortal coil: die.

This phrase that appears in *Hamlet* combines the archaic meaning of two words. "Shuffle" meant "rid," while "coil" meant "troubles." As Shakespeare put it, "What dreams may come / When we have shuffled off this mortal coil / Must give us pause."

⁂

sine qua non: essential part.

As translated from the Latin, "Without which, there would be nothing," the phrase is an erudite way to describe that which is indispensable or basic.

sitting on a powder keg: in imminent danger.

This phrase that arose in the early 19th century (if not before) suggests being atop a barrel of gunpowder that could explode at any time.

⁂

skin of your teeth: the narrowest of margins.

Job 19:20 has its protagonist say, "I am nothing but skin and bones; I have escaped with only the skin of my teeth." That is to say, Job's gums, the skin that held his teeth in place, which would indeed have been a narrow margin.

⁂

$64 question: the essential or ultimate question.

One of the most popular radio quiz shows during the 1940s was *Take It or Leave It* in which contestants strived to answer question after question until they reached the top prize of sixty-four silver dollars. The questions increased in difficulty, and at any point contestants could choose to stop and keep the amount of money they had won to that point. The phrase "$64 dollar question" became a catchword to the point that it became the program's name, and people applied the phrase to any very important question or matter.

Even more popular was the 1950s television spin-off, *The $64,000 Question*, with the phrase, now adjusted to inflation, catching on in popular speech, but not to the extent that its antecedent did.

skeleton in the closet: a hidden shame.

As if hiding a murder victim or another object that would cause great distress to the hider if found, to have a skeleton in the closet is to have a secret of any sort that you don't want revealed.

sliced bread: the last best thing.

An American inventor named Otto Rohwedder devised a machine that sliced a loaf of bread into individual slices. First sold in 1928, it was touted as "the greatest forward step in the baking industry since bread was wrapped," which led to popular phrase "the best thing since sliced bread."

All of which raises the question, what did people say before "sliced bread"? "The best thing since indoor plumbing" was one phrase. And before that?—"since powdered wigs?" "Since moveable type?" "Since fire?"

⌇

slow boat to China: a very long time.

A poker players' expression for a player who constantly lost was "I'd like to get you on a slow boat to China," meaning that the others would have all the time in the world to win the guy's money. Composer Frank Loesser used the phrase as the title and the first line of a 1948 romantic ballad, and the expression started being used as a compliment.

⌇

small potatoes: an inconsequential amount or insignificant item or matter.

Dating from the mid-19th century, the phrase suggests not bothering with undersized spuds while harvesting or buying the vegetable.

❧

sneak the sunrise past a rooster: attempt something that's impossible, or be slick enough to do something by stealth.

This predominantly Southern expression was famously used by California Angels first baseman Joe Adock, who said that "trying to sneak a pitch past [Atlanta Braves hitting great] Hank Aaron is like trying to sneak the sunrise past a rooster."

❧

"So's your old man!": The same to you, buddy!

Casting another's parent (the "Yo Mama" jokes) or parentage ("you son of a bitch!") in an unfavorable light has always been part of popular speech. "So's your old man!" is no more than a comeback that is used when (1) you don't want to provoke your antagonist very much or (2) you can't think of a more clever rejoinder.

You might have said "Aw, your mother wears combat boots," which, before women served in combat in the military, implied that she was less than feminine. That was a dangerous thing to do: fathers and other male relatives were fair game, but the female side of the family, and especially one's mother, was out of bounds before "Yo Mama" jokes crossed that boundary.

❧

sob sister: someone devoted to charities, or (less charitably) a do-gooder.

Originally a newspaper reporter or editor, invariably a woman, whose assignment was to produce sentimental stories and interviews that would appeal to female readers. By extension, the phrase came to mean any overly emotional person, whether male or female, especially one involved in charitable and public service efforts where sad tales of the recipients would tug on their heartstrings.

❧

social butterfly: a person who flits from event to event without a care in the world.

This derogatory phrase is usually but not always applied to women who "live to party." Going from one dinner party or ball or benefit to another, they are preoccupied with being the height of fashion and popularity. According to one wonderfully descriptive characterization, a social butterfly has a "brow unfurrowed by care or thought."

sock hop: a school dance.

Back in the days when school dances were held in gymnasiums, students were requested to remove their shoes, which would otherwise scratch the varnished and polished floor. It being the bobby-sox era, kids Lindy-hopped and slow-danced in their socked feet, and the events became known as sock hops.

&

soda jerk: drug story counterman.

Those of us old to remember when pharmacies sold nothing but medicine and medications, magazines and comic books, candy, and soda fountain treats, a man behind the zinc-and-marble counter made and dispensed sodas, frappes, milkshakes, malteds, and other ice cream–based concoctions, as well as banana splits, Cokes, lime rickeys, and dozens of other refreshments.

He was the soda jerk, the name coming from the fountain dispensers with handles that he jerked down to pour seltzer and other soft drinks.

For some unclear reason, women weren't soda jerks.

&

sound as a dollar: very safe.

There was a time when the American dollar was the cornerstone of the world's economy, a dependable currency to be admired and aspired to by other nations.

That was then, but global economic circumstances have changed. 'Nuff said.

❧

the sow that eats its farrow: Ireland.

The phrase comes from James Joyce's *Portrait of the Artist as a Young Man:* "Do you know what Ireland is? asked Stephen with cold violence. Ireland is the old sow that eats her farrow."

A "farrow" is a litter of newborn piglets, and the reference is Joyce's belief that Ireland had a history of destroying its writers, admirable political figures, and indeed everything that should be saved and nurtured.

❧

speak of the devil: acknowledgment of someone's unexpected arrival.

The complete expression is "speak of the devil and he will appear," which is nothing that superstitious people wanted to have happen. As such a cautionary tale, the expression was not used in jest until the late 19th century. That's when responding to an unanticipated appearance with "speak of the devil" lost its dark satanic connotation.

৵

spic and span: neat and clean.

A "spick" was a nail (as in "spike"), "span" was a wood shaving, and a new wooden object had shiny spicks in it and fresh spans around it. Over the years the meaning of newness was replaced by that of something fresh and clean (as a new object usually was).

৵

spin the bottle: a kissing game.

A weekend party of adolescents. The living room or playroom was darkened and a bunch of girls and boys sat around a circle. A boy placed an empty cola bottle on the floor in the center of the ring and spun it. The bottle stopped, its neck pointed at a girl—whom the guy got to kiss! Then it was the girl's turn . . .

Ah, for the days of such innocent kissing games as "Spin the Bottle" and "Post Office" (two groups in different rooms, each person goes to the other room and kisses members of the opposite sex), where the worst that the participants could expect was to be an embarrassing surprise visit from parents or chaperon.

⌘

spit in the ocean: an inconsequential amount.

The image is a single expelled moist mouthful being nothing compared to the entirely watery content of the Atlantic or Pacific.

A similar phrase is "a drop in the bucket."

⌘

square peg in a round hole: a misfit.

Its origin attributed to the 19th-century British philosopher and cleric Sydney Smith, the phrase has been used in a business context to describe someone who doesn't fit in to corporate culture, isn't a team player, and therefore stands little chance of corporate advancement.

⌘

stag line: unattached men at a dance.

Men who had no date for a dance but still wanted to go would stand along one wall and either ask unattached women to dance or cut in on a couple that was dancing.

Going stag to a dance had no unpleasant connotation. Not so for unattached females, known as "wallflowers." True or not, wallflowers were suspected of not being popular enough to attract a date.

❧

start from scratch: start at the beginning with no advantage.

The scratch line was a stripe across the ground where a race began. Starting from scratch meant having no advantage against others in the race where handicaps allowed some entrants shorter distances to run.

❧

straight arrow: a conventional and ethical person.

As morally straight as an arrow, that person is likely to be dull. As used in colleges during the mid-20th century, a straight arrow wasn't the type who'd get drunk or use drugs. If female, her necking, petting, or going further was out of the question.

❧

status seeker: someone who aspires to a higher socioeconomic level.

Upward mobility have always been an aspect of American society, but it took sociologist Vance Packard's 1959 book *The Status Seekers* to give a name to people who strove to impress by acquiring and flaunting fashionable and expensive items and social cachet. Status seekers—the derogatory epithet quickly gained popularity—not only tried to keep up with the Jones, they wanted to leave the Jones behind.

᪐

stew zoo: an apartment house in which many female flight attendants lived.

Back in prepolitically correct days, female flight attendants were called "stewardesses" and had the reputation for being attractive and, even better to the male mind, "fun" (Frank Sinatra's hit ballad "Come Fly with Me" became something of an anthem).

Stewardesses (or a many self-styled hip males called them "stewardii") shared apartments, a rent-saving arrangement that appealed to their lifestyle because one or more was usually traveling. Apartment buildings in large cities, especially ones with easy access to airports, that attracted the young women were known as "stew zoos."

᪐

stop, look, and listen: railroad crossing warning.

Before the installation of gates and flashing lights, a road that crossed a railroad track had a post on which was an X. On the crossbars was written "stop look listen," a phrase attributed to an anonymous engineer who through that immigrants who read only rudimentary English would be able to understand the three words and heed their warning.

Now automatic devices warn motorists and pedestrians to be mindful of approaching trains.

❧

Stop the music! Hold everything!

Stop The Music was a popular radio quiz show that began in 1947 and moved to television a year later. Studio contestants and home listeners or viewers (by telephone) heard a song played, then try to be the first one to guess its title. As soon as contestants indicated that they knew the answer, emcee Burt Parks shouted the show's title.

Thanks to the program, anyone who wanted to break into a conversation to make a point or to get someone's attention yelled "stop the music!"

Stop the presses! Hold everything!

Back in the days when newspapers were a more important and timely source of national and international happenings than they now are, their publishers made every effort to update news articles, even if it meant halting the printing process for a piece to be added or rewritten. When that happened, the cry "stop the presses" was heard, and the presses ground to a halt in mid-issue.

You didn't have to be Perry White or Citizen Kane to shout "stop the presses!" All you had to do was mean you were about to say something of importance or, when meant sarcastically, to indicate that another person's statement was old news.

---

the straw that broke the camel's back: the final limit of capacity, including patience.

An Arabian anecdote told of a camel whose owner loaded the beast of burden with as much straw as possible. Not satisfied with the staggering load he had put on the camel, the owner added just one last piece of straw. Even that one wisp was too much, and the animal collapsed with a broken back, leaving the owner with no way to take his goods to the market.

The story is a parable for all the times you've been repeatedly irked until you can't take it anymore and you explode.

⟡

struggle buggy: the backseat of a car.

This early- and mid-20th-century expression described an auto whose young owner tried to seduce unwilling young women into its backseat for a little (one of the euphemisms for the activity was "backseat boogie").

As the sophomoric joke went, "I call my car the Mayflower because so many Puritans came across in it."

⟡

Sunday-go-to-meeting clothes: best finery.

Churchgoers never wore their everyday clothing to worship service. Instead, they wore their Sunday best, their Sunday-go-to-meeting clothes.

⟡

S.W.A.K. (sealed with a kiss): a mark of affection on the back of an envelope.

Before e-mail, Facebook, and Twitter, people exchanged romantic sentiments by means of handwritten letters. One way to include a final bit of tenderness was to write S.W.A.K. on the back of the envelope.

Women often blotted their lipstick over the four letters to emphasize their love.

❧

swan song: last effort.

An ancient belief held that swans, who are usually silent, burst into beautiful song with their dying breaths. As a phrase, "swan song" connotes a last burst of energy before expiring.

❧

sword of Damocles: an imminent and/or constant threat.

According to Greek legend, Damocles, a friend of King Dionysius of Syracuse, envied the ruler's great wealth and power. When Damocles told the king how fortunate he was, Dionysius offered to change places for a day.

As Damocles dined at the head of the table, he happened to look up. There above his head, held by only a single horsehair, hung a sharp sword pointing downward toward his chair. Frozen with fear that the thread would break, he pointed out the predicament to the king.

❧

Dionysius nodded, acknowledging that the sword was a constant factor in his life, an actual and a metaphoric reminder that some person or circumstance might at any time cut the thread. Such risk, the king added, comes as an integral part of power.

Any ever-present risk, especially one that's hanging by a thread, is how the phrase has been used.

⌘

T

table d'hôte: a set menu at a fixed price.

Back in the days when America's idea of gracious dining was French cuisine (and therefore French terminology), upscale restaurants offered two choices in the way diners could order meals. One, which survives, is a là carte, where dishes were ordered and paid for individually.

The other was *table d'hôte* (literally, the host's table). That was a set menu offering little or no choice of appetizer, entrée, and dessert, and all for a fixed amount of money. *Table d'hôte* had its origin in the days when traveler stopped at an inn and dined on whatever the innkeeper's wife was serving as the family dinner.

⌘

The idea continues as prix fixe (fixed price) meals, for only rarely if ever and even at French restaurants will you find the phrase *"table d'hôte"* on a menu.

❧

Take a powder!: Scram!

This tough-guy phrase came from the days when a ladies' bathroom was euphemistically called the powder room, the place where women went, among other reasons, to apply makeup. As gangster movies would have us believe, a lady's escort who wanted to discuss a matter in privacy with another gent told her to "take a powder." Similarly, a genteel way to say you were going to the ladies' room was "I'm going to powder my nose."

❧

take one for the team: to make a sacrifice on behalf of the group.

The "classic" use of the phrase is when a baseball batter deliberately allows himself to be hit by a pitched ball that forces a home run to win a tied game.

Another scenario: your pal wants to go out on a date with a real babe, but the babe won't go unless your pal finds a date for her homely friend. Your pal begs you. You accept. You're taking one for the team.

⁓

take two and hit to right: I have no idea what you should do.

This baseball expression means that the batter should let the first two pitches go by and hit to the right side of the diamond. Why the batter should let what might be perfectly hittable pitches go by has never been explained, and neither has the phrase's origin.

The expression entered general use as something to say when you are asked for advice for which you have no better answer. You feel as though to have to say something, so you say "take two and hit to right." Your listener will either nod knowingly and say "thanks a lot" or stare blankly at you until you explain what you meant.

⁓

teacher's pet: someone who seeks preferential treatment.

A derisive epithet hurled at a student who tries to curry a teacher's favor in hopes of a better grade. Such a charge, valid or not, often led to cloakroom or schoolyard challenges and bloody noses.

Outside of school, it was applied to people who insinuated themselves to authority in the hope of special treatment.

The French equivalent is "teacher's little cabbage."

❧

"Tell it to the marines": a scornful response to an unbelievable story.

Beginning in the 17th century, marines were land forces who were stationed on ships of the Royal Navy. As landlubbers, they were understandably naive if not ignorant about life aboard a vessel and on the waves. Sailors took advantage and concocted outlandish stories that the marines swallowed hook, line, and sinker.

Accordingly, any outlandish story heard on land or sea and recognized as bilge was greeted with the full rejoinder, "You may tell that to the marines, but the sailors will not believe it," subsequently shortened over generations to "Aw, tell it to the marines!"

❧

"Tennis anyone?"

A convention of British drawing room comedies and certain novels of the 1920s and '30s was a brainless but good-natured upper-class twit—think P.G. Wodehouse's Bertie Wooster—who would appear in white flannels (*de rigeur* for tennis in those days), brandish his racquet, and inquire among the other weekend house-party guests, "Anyone for tennis?"

The phrase caught on, as such mindless clichés are wont to do, and decades of wannabe-clever young men on both sides of the Atlantic who felt obliged to say something—anything—would ask, "Tennis, anyone?" even if there weren't a court within miles . . . and then they wondered why no one laughed.

❧

three sheets to the wind: very drunk.

Despite what it sounds like to nonsailors, a "sheet" isn't a sail. It's the rope that secures the sail's edge or corner to the mast or the vessel itself. A sheet that comes loose flaps erratically, much like a drunken sailor weaving his way back to the ship after a night's alcoholic revelry. Three sheets blowing in the wind would be even worse.

❧

throw down the gauntlet: issue a challenge.

In the Middle Ages a gauntlet was the glove in a suit of armor. Throwing down his gauntlet was a knight's way to challenge an opponent to combat.

❧

throw in the towel (or sponge): to quit.

A prizefighter's sidemen use sponges to clean his face of sweat and blood. To toss the sponge into the ring during a fight signaled that the boxer had had enough—and so the sponge was no longer needed.

In recent years, towels have been substituted for sponges in boxing matches, and consequently, in the expression too.

༼ཉ

"Throw me a bone!": help!
College students used this phrase to ask classmates for assistance in studying for an exam or as a request for the answers.

༼ཉ

tied to his mother's apron strings: Momma's boy.
An adult male deeply attached to his mother, dating from the era when mothers (and other home-makers and housekeepers) wore aprons.

༼ཉ

tilt at windmills: fight imaginary enemies or fight a battle that can't be won.
"Tilt" means "joust," as in mounted knights fight-ing each other with lances. In Miguel Cervantes's *Don Quixote*, the Man of La Mancha came upon a row of windmills and took them for giants, their flailing arms ready to do battle. Despite his squire

Sancho Panza's pointing out that they were wind-mills, Don Quote set his lance, spurred his steed Rocinante, and charged the "enemy." Alas for the Knight of the Woeful Countenance, the windmills prevailed.

Anyone who similarly takes on a losing cause is tilting at windmills.

⌘

tinhorn gambler: an unsuccessful player.

In the dice game of chuck-a-luck, backroom play-ers tossed the dice not with their hand but out of a small metal handheld cage called the "horn" (more upscale games used leather horns). Hence, the "tin horn" noun that became the "tinhorn" adjective when applied to nickel-dime gamblers.

"Tinhorn" sounds as though it might also refer to a musical instrument, and composer Frank Loesser took advantage of that sound-alike association with "Fugue for Tinhorns" in his musical *Guys & Dolls*.

⌘

tinker's damn: something of no value.

Itinerant tinsmiths known as tinkers were rough-and-ready men who saw no reason to watch their language. They swore so frequently that their curse words had no value for emphasis or anything else, and so something that was said to be worth a tinker's damn had no merit or value at all.

❧

Tom Swifty: a punning word game.

Tom Swift was the hero of a series of boys' adventure books first published in 1910. Author Victor Apppleton rarely used the word "said" without adding adverbs, a style that someone turned into a word game in which punsters add adverbs that suit what Tom is saying.

Classic examples of Tom Swiftys (or Swifties) are "Sesame," said Tom openly; "I only use one herb when I cook," said Tom sagely; and "I swallowed some of the glass from that broken window," Tom said painfully.

❧

top banana: headliner comedian in a vaudeville show.

The phrase is said to have originated with a vaudevillian named Harry Steppe in 1927 from a skit in which three comics tried to figure out how to share two bananas.

Steppe also claimed to have first used "second banana" to refer to the cast's number 2 comic.

Comedian Phil Silvers popularized the phrase "Top Banana" when he used it as the title of his Broadway musical and movie.

❧

top drawer: highest quality.

The 19th-century practice of keeping jewelry and other valuables in the highest drawer of a bedroom dresser gave rise to this phrase, which was applied both to people and to things.

"First rate" is a similar phrase, as is "varsity," meaning a person figuratively sufficiently admirable to qualify for the starting team.

❧

touch and go: a risky situation.

There are times when a ship's captain or pilot must pick the vessel's way through such a narrow channel that its sides might well scrape against rocks or other potentially destructive hazards. Nevertheless, the captain or pilot had no other choice. That is to say, the ship might touch but it had to go regardless of the risk. Hence, this expression for an uncertain enterprise.

A literal application of the phrase is an airplane's touching down on the runway, but then immediately lifting off because a normal landing would be dangerous. Pilots practice the maneuver when learning to fly.

❦

town-gown: relations between a college and the municipality in which it is located.

Students at British universities and boarding schools were fond of playing pranks on the inhabitants of the cities and towns where the schools were. However, not all the "pranks" were pranks: drunken carousing, theft, arson, and other crimes were done under the guise of boyish high spirits.

These uneasy relations between town and "gown" (students wore academic robes, as in "cap and gown") happened in this country too, and there are still times when a mayor and a college dean meet to try and smooth ruffled feathers.

trip the light fantastic: dance.

The phrase comes from John Milton's poem "L'Allegro": "Come and trip it as ye go / On the light fantastic toe."

"Trip" did not mean to stub your toe and fall. On the contrary it meant "to move lightly and nimbly."

❦

tube steak: a humorous (and sometimes pretentious) name for a plain ol' hot dog.

have no truck with: avoid.

"Truck" came from the French woes for "barter." Originally, if you had no truck with somebody, you refused to trade with him or her. By extension it came to mean you refused to have anything to do with the person.

23-skiddoo!: Scram!

No one knows the origin of this phrase that started in the early 20th century. If it had started in the 1920s, when it was at its height of popularity, one might have thought it was a way to bid farewell to the year 1923. But both "23" and "skidoo" already existed as slang for getting out (or away) in a hurry.

Speculation about the origin includes the California mining town of Skidoo that had 23 saloons; going to town to hit them all might have been done without wasting time. Another thought is that construction workers at the Flatiron Building on Manhattan's West 23rd Street used the phrase to signal each other that an attractive young woman was passing.

But no one knows for sure.

two bits: 25 cents.

A unit of currency during the colonial era was the Spanish dollar coin, which was cut into eight pieces, each called a "bit." Dividing by four rather than eight was easier and led to change being made in two-bit increments. When the United States issued its own currency, the quarter became familiarly known as "two bits," a phrase that appears to be dying out.

It may well be best remembered for the high school and college cheer: "Two bits, four bits, six bits, a dollar / All for [name your school], stand up and holler" and for the musical tag "Shave an a haircut . . . two bits."

U

upper crust: the top level of society.

Although you might think that "crust" refers to bread and that the upper part was reserved for the aristocracy, word detectives would say you're wrong: no authoritative written connection between bread and the well-bred can be found. "Crust" refers to the earth's crust, or top layer. The upper crust of a society is its top layer.

up the river: in jail.

The infamous Sing Sing Correctional Facility, located in the town of Ossining thirty miles north of New York City, sits on the Hudson River shoreline. Any criminal convicted in a New York court and sentenced to be imprisoned there was sent "up the river."

The phrase, made popular in gangster movies, began to be applied to other prisons in the country, whether or not the cells boasted of a river view.

"Up the river" should not be confused with "sold down the river," meaning "deceived" and derived from the antebellum practice of Northern slaveholders selling troublesome slaves down the Mississippi River for a life of endless toil on cotton plantations.

up to scratch: meets the standards.

In the days of bare-knuckle fighting, bouts took place within a large circle drawn on the bare ground (that's where the phrase "boxing ring" came from). The contest began with the fighters facing off while standing on either side of a line scratched on the dirt in the middle of the ring.

A fighter who was physically and mentally ready to take part stood at the line and was, therefore, up to scratch.

"Up to snuff" has much the same meaning. Powdered tobacco was said to sharpen the user's mind, so if you were up to snuff, you were mentally and also physically ready to go.

❧

V

vaccinated with a Victrola needle: someone who chatters incessantly.

Victrola, a division of R.C.A. Victor, was a brand of phonograph players. Since phono records were played with needles that picked up the sound vibrations in the record's grooves, to be vaccinated with a Victrola needle, as the joke implied, was to be inoculated with the gift of nonstop gab.

❧

various and sundry: different and unspecified items.

"Various" means "several different things." So does "sundry" (variety stores sold sundry goods), so to report that "the meeting discussed various and sundry topics" is to be redundant. But that's never stopped all but the linguistically fastidious from using such expressions.

⁓

vim and vigor: full of vitality and enthusiasm.

Here's another redundant phase: "vim" comes from a Latin word for "stength," while "vigor" means the same thing. But alliteration carries the day, so if you're full of vim and vigor, you're hot to trot and go to go.

A similar expression is "piss 'n' vinegar," the latter word having long been used to mean a sharp vitality.

⁓

W

walking on eggs: being especially careful.

Even more than tiptoeing, the image of walking so gingerly that you wouldn't crack eggs is especially apt, for example, in broaching a sensitive subject, as in "When I brought up the subject of her ex-marriage, I felt as though I was walking on eggs."

⁓

warts and all: without spring any literal or figurative blemishes.

The phrase is attributed to England's Lord Protector Oliver Cromwell, who ordered Sir John Lely, the artist painting his portrait, not to flatter him, but to paint him with any and all physical imperfections . . . "'warts and all."

As many people over the years credited Cromwell with the phrase, there is no definite proof that he did indeed use it. Still, if he didn't, he should have.

෴

like water off a duck's back: without any apparent effect.

Ducks' feathers are waterproof. The preen (or, formally, the uropygial) gland at the base of the tail produces oil that spreads and covers the birds' outer coat so that water forms droplets on, but does not permeate, the feathers.

That's why a critical remark that doesn't bother the person for whom it was intended rolls off like water off a duck's back.

෴

wear your heart on your sleeve: reveal your emotions so that they are subject to the comments of others.

A young man who has a crush on a young lady may tell everyone that he can't live without her, even though his words may be met by his friends' sneers and jeers. If so, he's wearing his heart on his sleeve, which is to say exposing it in a vulnerable place.

The phrase comes from *Othello*, where devious Iago says,

For when my outward action doth demonstrate
The native act and figure of my heart

In compliment extern, 'tis not long after
But I will wear my heart upon my sleeve
For daws [ravens] to peck at. I am not what I am.

⌘

the weed of crime bears bitter fruit: no good will
come from criminal schemes.

The Shadow was a very popular radio detective
series that began in the early 1930s. Its hero, playboy
Lamont Cranston, had "the power to cloud men's
minds," a form of hypnosis by which he appeared off
to the side of where people thought he stood (contrary to popular belief, the Shadow did not make
himself invisible).

After the credits at the end of every episode, the
Shadow intoned, "The weed of crime bears bitter
fruit. Crime does not pay! The Shadow knows," and
then utter a sardonic laugh.

Another famous Shadow-ism was "Who knows
what evil lurks in the minds of men?—The Shadow
knows!"

⌘

wet blanket: a spreader of gloom.

What could put more of a damper on lovely summer day picnic than a wet ground cloth—unless it's a
person who, by word or deed, spoils everyone's fun?

Such a spoilsport at any otherwise enjoyable event goes by the epithet "wet blanket," better known to recent generations as a party pooper.

⁂

whirling dervish: boundless energy.

Dervishes are members of a mendicant religious order of Sufi Moslems. Part of their worship is a trance-inducing ritual in which the men, who wear billowing white skirts whirl in circles meant to replicate planets revolving around the sun.

"Whirling dervish" became a metaphor for nonstop energy, used in such ways as "He dashed through the hardware store, then ran home and cleaned out the garage and then built shelves along one wall, all before lunch—he was a regular whirling dervish."

⁂

white elephant: an expensive but useless possession.

Albino elephants are extremely rare, and any born in Siam became the property of the king. These favored specimens were not allowed to be worked or to be killed without the royal permission. As the story goes, the king often perversely gave a white elephant to a courtier who had fallen out of favor, just so the nobleman would spend a small fortune maintaining the useless gift for the rest of its life.

Rummage sales in which people donate items for which they (and possibly no one else) have no use are often called "white elephant sales."

❦

whole nine yards: the entire amount or distance.

Of all phrases in the English language, few have as many supposed sources as this one. Among the possibilities are the nine yards of material from which tailors made expensive men's suits; the nine cubic yards of concrete that concrete trucks held; the nine yards (or spars) on a three-masted sailing ship; the volume of grave soil; and the length of a World War II aircraft ammunition belt.

However, none of these or any other explanation has been conclusively proven. The phrase first appeared during the 1960s of out Vietnam War writings with no further explanation.

Other phrases that refer to everything are "all the marbles," "the whole shooting match," "the whole ball of wax," and "the whole shebang."

❦

widow's weeds: female mourning costume.

The word "weed" comes from an Old English word for "garment." As a phrase to wear widow's weeds simply means to be in mourning.

Many cultures have had or still have a custom of wearing distinctive clothing to mark a husband's death. In Victorian England, for example, a widow wore black for the first year and a day, then moved through dark purple and other somber colors to lighter shades.

However, the queen who gave her name to the era wore no other color than black after the death of her beloved husband Prince Albert. Many widows in many Mediterranean countries, most notable Greece and southern Italy, wear black for the rest of their lives.

⚬

wild goose chase: a hopeless search or pursuit.

The phrase comes from Shakespeare's *Romeo and Juliet*:

Romeo: Switch and spurs, switch and spurs; or I'll cry a match.

Mercutio: Nay, if thy wits run the wild-goose chase, I have done, for thou hastmore of the wild-goose in one of thy wits than, I am sure, I have in my whole five.

Although chasing a wild goose seems pointless and doomed to failure, Shakespeare's reference was to horse racing, where a "wild goose chase" was a race in which horses followed a lead horse at a set distance, mimicking wild geese flying in formation.

will o' the wisp: an unattainable goal.

Will o' the wisp is one of the names of the marsh gas phenomenon that causes lights suddenly to appear and disappear over swampy ground (ignis fatuus is another term). Trying to catch a will o' the wisp is impossible, much like trying to catch lightning in a bottle, and so the phrase came to mean anything that can't be done.

working stiff: a hardworking employee.

First heard in the 1930s, this phrase describes your average guy or gal who works at a not-very-interesting-or-stimulating job and for wages that mean a paycheck-to-paycheck existence.

"Stiff" might have come from muscle fatigues at the end of the day or week, but it's just as likely to be the slang word for "corpse," which would reflect the idea of a working stiff in a dead-end job.

the world is your oyster: anything you wish is yours for the taking.

This piece of advice, usually given to youngsters, suggests that their future holds great riches, the way an oyster contains a pearl, and all they need do is use education, skill, or another talent to pry open the metaphorical bivalve and claim their reward.

In Shakespeare's *The Merry Wives of Windsor*, the character Pistol is heard to say, "Why then the world's mine oyster / Which I with sword will open."

⁂

writer's cramp: a painful spasm in the hand that restricts the ability to use a pen or pencil.

Back in the Paleozoic Era when people wrote by hand instead of typewriters and then computers (you youngsters can ask your parents or grandparents if you don't believe me), excessive use of a pen or pencil would cause a person's hand to tense up or go into a spasm that made further writing painful or impossible or both.

The condition wasn't called "repetitive stress syndrome" back then. It was "writer's cramp," and that was no excuse for the schoolroom punishment of being made to write "I will not talk in class" one hundred times on the blackboard.

⁂

wrong side of the blanket: illegitimacy.

A child born out of wedlock was said to have been born on the wrong side of the blanket, as if being under the covers was a luxury to which only legitimate babies were entitled.

Other obsolescent phrases for an illegitimate baby are "natural child" and "love child."

⁂

wrong side of the tracks: the less desirable part of town.

In many 19th- and early-20th-century America, railroad tracks divided a city or town. On one side was the middle- and upper-class residential and commercial area. On the other were factories and residential shacks and tenements. Since residents of the former made class distinctions and applied appropriate language, anyone from the other part of town came from the wrong side of the tracks.

⁂

Y

Yankee ingenuity: intelligent self-reliance using available materials.

The phrase originated when mid-Atlantic and Southern colonists admired the ingenuity with which their New England neighbors were able to improvise tools and other ways to cope with poor farming conditions and harsh weather. Later on, and despite the dismay of sons and daughters of the Confederacy, "Yankee" described all of the United States (as in "The Yanks Are Coming"), and the phrase was similarly expanded to reflect American know-how and inventiveness.

❧

You're in the army now!: Shape up—things are done differently here.

One of the stock comedy bits in World War II movies was the rude awakening that recruits received during basic training. Any buck private who tried to oversleep or do anything else that wasn't according to military procedure would be chewed out by his drill sergeant, with an unceremonious, "Hey, you ain't no civilian no more, mister—you're in the army now!"

The phrase followed the soldiers home, and well into the '50s anyone who was corrected by an ex-GI was liable to be told, "Do it right, mister—you're in the army now!"

❧

yours truly: I.

For whatever reason of modesty (or false modesty) that prevented speakers or writers from using the first-person singular pronoun "I," the "yours truly" convention was established. It came from the standard letter closing. It sounded mannered when it was first used in the 19th century and even more so now.

Other equally stilted circumlocutions for "I" or "me" used in writing are "your reporter" (still found in alumni class notes) and "your correspondent."

⚭

Z

zoot suit: a man's ensemble for hipsters and other cool dudes.

Popular during the 1930s and '40s, a zoot suit featured a long coat with wide lapels and padded shoulders and matching high-waisted, ballooning pants. Fancy shoes and a felt fedora hat completed the hipster "look."

"Zoot" was apparently a variation of the word "suit."